C000172598

THIS BOOK IS DEDICATED TO
POPPY
A LOVELY GENTLE CREATURE,
HALF ROTTWEILER HALF GREAT
DANE, WHO COMPETELY RULES OUR
HOUSE - AND KNOWS IT!

THE SHOW BEGINS...

If it hadn't been for a hot summer's afternoon and the fact that I had taken more time than usual browsing round a second-hand book-shop somewhere in Charing Cross Road, this story might never have been written. Rummaging through old books can be a fascinating hobby, especially if you have sufficient money to purchase one. On this occasion I had, which was more than could be said for the shifty looking gentleman who was also in the shop and who, for some strange reason sported a mackintosh on this very warm day. The garment, in turn, appeared to be bulging in peculiar places and at odd angles.

The owner of the shop having disappeared for a few minutes, gave the shifty looking man the chance he had been waiting for. Peering left then right, he bolted through the exit door, never to be seen again, nor I fear, were the volumes hidden beneath his mac.

I had been so intrigued watching this man at work that I had not realised how time was slipping by. It was nearly 5.30 pm and I was going to be late for my next appointment. Hurriedly, I swung round to make for the door and as I did so, sent a book flying. As I bent to pick it up, I had little thought this book was to alter the whole course of my life. The book was called *Houdini*. I tucked it under my arm, paid a few shillings for it, which is something I recommend the shifty gentleman to try sometime, and marched out of the shop. So this was my introduction to the Great Houdini, the man, some of whose feats, in later years, I tried to imitate.

Today, in my capacity as a professional escapologist and stuntman, I get asked many strange questions by many strange people. The question, quite naturally perhaps, which I am asked more than any other is: What made you start this sort of thing? Well that's the answer, the little book I knocked to the ground in a small bookshop in the West End of London.

SAILING
DOWN
THE RIVER

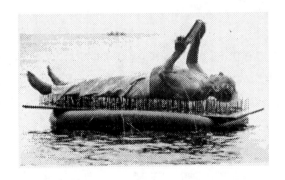

IN THIS STORY I am describing a few of the amusing and – in some cases – exciting stunts that I have performed; but this does not constitute an autobiography: just some episodes from a fairly large selection which, in turn, will introduce one or two of the interesting personalities who it has been my good fortune to meet.

We cannot do better than to begin at the beginning, and so we turn back the hands of the clock and indeed, the pages of the calendar, to find ourselves sailing up the River Thames on an ancient, but proud paddle-steamer, going under the majestic name of *The Empress of India,* which the reader may note is almost as majestic as my own stage name – The Great Omani!

The passengers on this outing consisted of a rather beery crowd of gentlemen with their equally 'ginny' wives; and if music be the food of love, then they must have been well-nourished. Their voices were raised in happy song and even if they did scare the birds for miles around, everyone was having a rollicking good time; with the exception, that is, of one person – myself. I had promised the organisers of this party that I would come along and 'do a turn' for them; and the 'turn' I had in mind was to leap from the boat into the river whilst *chained and handcuffed.* In fact, to give my first public performance for the astronomical fee of twenty-five shillings and free beer!

As the boat drew nearer to Marlow, the place selected for the entertainment, I began to wonder if it was such a good idea after all.

True, I had studied and trained carefully in the art of underwater escapology in the shallow-end of a swimming pool, but now, for the first time, I was up against the real thing. The Thames looked very deep, and the current very swift, as I confided my fears to Marvita, my wife, who had been trained to put the handcuffs and chains on. Her reply that 'You can only drown once,' did not, so far as I could see, in any way help the situation. Her second suggestion, that a double gin might help, was far more practical and promptly acted upon.

'Well, it's nearly time; we're almost there,' said the organiser of the party. 'Where would you like to dive from?' 'Are you sure they want this sort of thing?' I croaked, 'I mean, they seem so happy singing. It's a pity to interrupt them for a little show like mine.' 'Nonsense!' said the organiser. 'We wouldn't miss a stunt like this for the world; would we, Bill?' Bill, who had just joined the party, agreed that everybody would be disappointed if they didn't see the stunt – and that we just had time for a 'quick one' before they dropped anchor.

Now it was time to go on. I swallowed the drink quickly, changed into my swimming trunks and, grabbing my chains and handcuffs in one hand and Marvita in the other, made towards the part of the boat chosen for the Big Stunt. *The Empress of India* had dropped anchor; I stood ready on the diving-stage, overhanging the side of the ship. The organiser suddenly held up his hands. 'Ladies and Gentlemen.' he yelled. 'May I have your attention, if you please? I am not one for making speeches ...' 'Then shut up!' yelled a gentleman with a large red nose, the magnificent hue of which could only have been achieved through persistent and excessive drinking. 'Shut up, yourself,' yelled somebody in the background. 'You talking to me, mate?' came the reply, and before we knew where we were, tempers were running high, pushes were about to turn into blows, and I had visions of other people disappearing over the side of the ship as well as me.

'Start chaining me up, Marvita!' I said. 'Quick!' Swiftly and efficiently she curled the long chain round my body; slipping numerous locks on as she went. 'Look!' shouted one of the women, 'She's chaining the bloke up.' Suddenly, their heads began to turn towards us and as the chains continued to curl around my body, I noted we were fast gaining their undivided attention. Click, click, as Marvita snapped the handcuffs on. There was an excited stir which ran through the audience. 'Cripes,' said the woman again, ''E's potty!'

'Ladies and Gentlemen,' shouted the organiser again, this time being determined not to be done out of his speech. 'As I was about to say when I was interrupted, this young man, Mr Omani, will now jump into the river and attempt to free himself underwater from his shackles. This daring feat has been arranged especially for your entertainment.' I bowed to the audience the best way I could and took my position on the diving-platform. 'Are you ready?' shouted Marvita. 'No!' I snapped. 'Wait until that swan has gone past?' 'It *has* gone,' said Marvita. I looked, hoping that another would rapidly appear, but it was not to be. 'You can't put it off any longer,' she hissed, 'they're all watching you.' 'All right.' I shouted, 'Ready!' and closed my eyes. With a great deal of encouragement from Marvita in the form of a severe push, I found myself falling rapidly through the air. As I opened my eyes I saw Old Father Thames rushing up to meet me, then SPLASH! The next thing I knew, I was lying on some gravel at the bottom of the river. My feet appeared to be securely chained and my wrists handcuffed. This might have been the end of this chapter and indeed the end of me. Luckily, however, my early and previous training stood me in good stead. Quickly and methodically, I went to work, first releasing my wrists and then on to the locks, one by one, until the last of them was open and the chains fell loosely beside me on the gravel. Slowly, I began to feel my body rise. At the same time a thrill ran through me and now not even the cold water could dampen my ardour. I had done it: my first professional turn! Was I not the greatest escapologist in the country, and probably the world?

My thoughts soon scattered as my head came slowly above the water again. As I shook the water from my eyes I saw two hundred heads craning over the side of the boat. Two hundred pairs of hands applauded loudly. I had done it, and had been one minute and ten seconds underwater. I swam to the side of the boat, and was promptly hauled aboard amidst much clapping and shouting. I made my most spectacular bow. The stunt had been a big hit; of that there could be no question.

As *The Empress of India* sailed back that evening to Windsor with her tired but happy party, I noticed how big and yet how beautiful the castle looked, silhouetted as it was against a background of dark blue sky. Here and there, flights of birds wheeled, racing in search of a resting place before the sun disappeared into the mysterious depths of the heavens, to give place to a regular visitor to the night sky: the twinkling Evening Star. The cries of happy children, splashing in the water before returning home from their day at the river, reached my ears. Yes, it had been a good day for many people, that sunny August Saturday.

Suddenly, I noticed an old lady beckoning to me. As I went over to her, she placed something in my hand. 'A wonderful show, young man,' she said. 'Really wonderful. You may become famous one day, but take care it doesn't kill you.'

Well, at the moment, I'm still alive and the little green cross she had pressed into my hand is still with me. I like to hold it when faced with a dangerous stunt; also as a memento of a kind old lady.

HASTINGS TO
PICCADILLY BY
COFFIN

YOU KNOW THE old saying, don't you, which runs some thing like this: 'It wasn't the cough that carried him off; t'was the coffin they carried him off in'? Well, that's just what happened to me. I was carried off in a coffin all the way from Hastings to Piccadilly Circus – I'll tell you about it.

I was once again racking my brain, trying to think up a new stunt, possibly an endurance test with (and this is always important) a danger angle attached to it. But what it was going to be for the life of me I had no idea; and to this day I'm not sure what eventually gave me the idea, but somehow it came to me. Supposing I travelled, I thought, from Hastings to Piccadilly Circus, lying in an open coffin stripped to the waist, lying on broken glass on top of a car and in mid-winter. Surely here was a real endurance test!

Could one travel all those miles, I wondered, in mid-winter without freezing to death? The fact of lying bareback all the way on the broken glass added yet another danger angle; and the mere sight of my jet black coffin would just complete the picture. The more I thought over this idea, the more I liked it. It had all the makings of a good publicity stunt and it had never been done before. This required one other person – someone with a car which had a sufficiently strong roof to hold my coffin. The driver would have to be a good showman. I knew of one man who would fit the bill admirably, his name was Professor Cullen and one of the greatest showmen I know. The professor owned just the right type of car and being an excellent showman had useful connections with the press.

14

Perhaps at this stage I should tell you a little more about the professor, for a more colourful character it would be hard to meet, and as we have worked together on several publicity stunts you will see his name mentioned several times before you arrive at the end of this book; and if you do arrive at the end of this book, dear reader, it will mean that you too have faced an endurance test. In this particular stunt he played an important part.

I had chosen my companion well for the professor was a show unto himself. To start with, he was Irish in every sense of the word. He had a generous Irish heart but, when aroused, the temper of Satan. At a very early age he joined the Queen's Regiment and spent about twenty years soldiering in India and China. During his stay in the Far East he studied some of the mysteries of the East, also palmistry and astrology. He wound up by becoming regimental sergeant-major, quite an achievement, in a famous regiment. Today the professor stands six feet tall with a red beard, and with long flowing dark hair down to his broad shoulders; and here you have a man who in many ways resembles 'Buffalo' Bill Cody. Much more I could tell you about the professor; sufficient to say however, that today he is a highly-skilled palmist and indeed a highly successful one. He has read, (amazingly accurately) the hands of some of the greatest stars in Europe. One thing more I will tell you – I know nobody who has a greater capacity for drinking beer than this man. He appears to be a human reservoir for alcoholic beverage! This is then the man I chose to be my partner.

That evening in a pub called The Silverhill Tavern I laid my plans before the professor. He listened carefully, interrupting only to order numerous bottles of beer which disappeared almost as quickly as they appeared. 'If only we could pull it off, it would be our biggest stunt yet,' I told him. 'If...what do you mean, if?' cried the irate professor, hitting the table with a resounding blow which made a lot of empty glasses jump in the air (as well as me). 'There is no such word as if. We will do it!' And once again in a most decisive manner his fist hit the table and the glasses and bottles jumped in the air. From that moment on the decision was made. 'We will drink on it.' said the professor – and that meant everybody in the bar! Drinks were pulled up at his expense. He raised his glass and called for order. 'Gentlemen,' he said. 'We will drink to Omani, the gamest boy in the country. He will travel from Hastings to Piccadilly in a coffin, lying on broken glass.' The rest of what happened that night has little bearing on this chapter. It is sufficient to say – glasses were filled; glasses were emptied to be filled again. The professor decided to give us a number of songs which is a habit of his in pubs. The customers all joined in and, in the words of the song, 'The music went round and round' – and for that matter, so did everything that stood in front of me.

It was decided that we would attempt the strange journey on Saturday, February First, and if the professor, the coffin and I finished the course we would drive to the BBC and relate our experiences to the world on the BBC programme *In Town Tonight*. I prayed that the weather would be as warm as possible on that day. However, this time my prayers were answered by the gathering of snow clouds on roofs and tops of trees, and as far as the eye could see there was a vast expanse of whiteness. England was in the grip of ice and snow. One of the coldest spells to hit the country for a number of years had arrived. 'This is wonderful,' beamed the professor. 'It puts the value of the stunt up. We'll have a few practice runs and get the press to take some shots of you in the snow. First, we'll take a run to Eastbourne and get the local press on it.' This we did next day but although the Eastbourne cameramen and reporters met us, nothing appeared in the Eastbourne papers. A half-naked man running around the countryside in a coffin was not the type of publicity this charming seaside resort was after. However, the Hastings and Brighton papers went to work on it. One paper wrote:

Sprinkling jagged pieces of glass into a coffin, the Hastings escapologist and stuntman The Great Omani said, 'There are only about a dozen broken bottles in at the moment. I shall need at least another dozen.' He was preparing for his biggest ever test of endurance. He plans to ride in the coffin on top of a car all the way to London. Whatever the weather he will be stripped to the waist resting his bare back on the mattress of broken glass. To sustain himself on the way he intends to chew a few electric-light bulbs.

This uncomfortable journey will take place on February First. When he arrives in London his experiences will be broadcast on *In Town Tonight.* His driver will be his friend the palmist and astrologer, Professor Patrick Cullen, who predicts 'I think it will be very cold that day.' But Omani does not mind. 'I shall keep myself warm with yoga methods,' he said. In the picture the Great Omani and Professor Cullen are preparing for a practice run.

My friend Mr Sidney Mayer, owner of the Dorian Hotel nearly opposite Hastings Pier, had decided to throw a party in our honour just before we started on our journey. As well as our personal friends, the press were to be invited to join the celebrations. Food and drink were to be supplied by Mr Mayer and a good time would be had by all. This appealed greatly to the professor. The morning of February First arrived and we all foregathered at eleven o'clock in the well decorated bar at the Dorian Hotel. The place was full; several members of the press were there. I noticed quite a number of Hastings and St Leonards publicans were present. Most of them, I suspected, were personal friends of the professor. A few of the local 'bigwigs' mingled with the crowd in the hope that the cameramen would take their pictures; and many others were milling around hoping to get as many free drinks as possible. Sidney Mayer, our host (who by the way is an Indian) did us all well, supplying as well as drinks, some delicious curried snacks. This I thought an excellent idea, and swallowed enormous quantities of Sidney's curry. If, I thought, I'm about to be cold on the outside, I may as well get warm on the inside. Toasts were drunk to the professor and myself wishing us good luck and 'bon voyage'. The professor and I, in turn, found it necessary to drink everybody's health and indeed, had the professor had his way we would have been the most healthy gathering in England.

18

It was time for us to start our strange pilgrimage; in fact it was well past our scheduled time for starting. I went up and changed into a pair of black trousers which were supported by a long scarlet sash round my waist, the end of which hung down my side. I was doing my best to look like some mystic person from the East. Diligently I climbed onto the top of the car and even more diligently lowered my behind into my coffin, the bottom of which sparkled with broken glass. The cameramen went to work taking shots of me from different angles. When they were finished I crossed my arms on my chest, appeared to go into a self-imposed hypnotic trance and slowly and mysteriously sank back into the coffin of broken glass. The professor shook hands with the local bigwigs and entered his driving seat; the car began to move and we were on our way.

As Hastings disappeared behind us I was aware of two things. One was that I was feeling damned cold on the outside and due to Sidney's curry, damned hot on the inside; and if I was permitted one other thought, it was that glass is most uncomfortable stuff to lie on, whether you're a yogi or not! My train of thoughts soon led me to ask myself why I spent my spare time thinking up these atrociously uncomfortable stunts? This I decided would be the last. I was now lying down as flat as I could so that most of the wind would pass over me and before long the professor was heading towards the town of Tonbridge. Somehow I had covered thirty miles on this strange ride.

The cold had already bitten well into me. I was doubtful, very doubtful, as to whether I could finish the course. Before long the professor pulled the car up outside a pub. 'You need a brandy,' he called. 'Hop down, we both need a brandy.' How right he was! 'Ten minutes only then we must be off.' 'It isn't every day,' said the barmaid, 'that people walk into this bar in the winter half naked and with bits of glass sticking out of their backs!' We hastily explained to this jovial wench what was happening. Soon the ten minutes were up and the military side of the professor became evident. 'Time to go,' boomed the ex-regimental sergeant-major; and so in (I'm glad to say) an orderly fashion we retreated back to the car. Outside quite a little crowd had gathered to have a look at us; something which never fails to satisfy both the professor and me. I mounted to the top of the car, settled down once again, and we were headed for London and the BBC.

Time they say marches on; sometimes very slowly it seems. Eventually however we arrived at the outskirts of London; and now I was holding on for dear life. I didn't want to give up on the last lap. Up to now I have omitted to tell you that I was carrying a letter of 'goodwill' from the landlord of the Jenny Lind, High Street, Hastings – who was none other than the British and Empire heavy-weight champion, Don Cockell – to the landlord of a pub in the Old Kent Road (another British boxer, Joe Lucey). This made me the first coffin postman in history! As the car arrived outside Lucey's pub I was in a pretty poor condition both physically and mentally and was helped down into the warm atmosphere of Joe's bar. I had never met Lucey before but was glad to do so now as he seemed to be a very nice fellow. So much so that we agreed to return that evening and make a short appearance for his customers.

And now it was time for the last lap, Piccadilly was near at hand – through Westminster and Trafalgar Square and we would be there. Eventually I heard the distant buzz of Piccadilly Circus. As we passed Pall Mall a strange feeling swept over me for I could see my father's old club just as it used to be when he was alive, where as a boy or young man I used to meet and lunch with him. I could picture myself with the bowler hat and neatly rolled umbrella, mounting the steps of the club which used to be (and no doubt still is) the rendezvous of the military coteries. Possibly my dear father had hopes that one day I too might become a member of this exclusive Pall Mall Club. So perhaps it was as well he couldn't see me passing by in my coffin – and without my bowler hat too!

Another two minutes and I had completed the journey. As the car entered Piccadilly Circus I slowly rose up out of the coffin with my arms crossed on my chest. As the traffic lights held us up for a minute the crowds quickly gathered and gaped. And no wonder, for never before had anyone travelled round Eros stripped to the waist on a biting February afternoon, sitting in an open coffin. Suddenly out of the corner of my eye I saw a sergeant and three policemen marching sternly towards us. Just before they arrived the lights changed from red to green and we were on our way. We circled Eros twice, much to the astonishment of the gaping crowd; the professor was all for another run round but I had other ideas. We shot off down Shaftesbury Avenue and turned into a side street. Stiffly I crawled out of the coffin with my teeth chattering. Shivering I leapt into my warm clothes. Clothes, I thought, as I shook from head to foot with cold, are far too much taken for granted and not sufficiently appreciated. Anyway, I had done it at last.

I slipped into a cafe for a tea while the professor stood on the pavement outside distributing 'Come to Hastings' brochures and answering questions about the trip. Knowing him to be an excellent 'spieler' I have no doubt that he was telling the innocent looking bystanders that my remarkable achievement was due to the Hastings sea air! I only hope that the Hastings publicity department appreciated that too!

With the journey successfully completed the next part of our programme was our visit to the BBC. Eventually it was our turn to take our seats opposite the microphones; John Ellison interviewed us and we supplied the answers to his questions. I finished up by demonstrating how to eat an electric light bulb; the sound effect of which proved most effective – if not the taste. And so, John Ellison brought our interview to a close. Another voice rang out 'Carry on London' and the programme came to another successful end. The professor and I decided there and then that we were by far the best turn on the programme; however that meant nothing because we always do imagine this!

In the early part of this chapter I told you that Cullen was a remarkable man; this I was about to find out. We had agreed (luckily not under contract) to appear that night at certain clubs in the West End of London; and indeed I had every intention of doing so. 'But first,' said the professor, 'we will go and see Vera.' And the next thing I knew, the car was pulling up outside a house in Bermondsey in the heart of dockland. 'Where,' pointed out the professor, 'they'd cut your throat for half-a-crown if they didn't like you.' I hoped they would like me. 'A man can disappear completely in these parts,' continued the professor 'if they like you and you're on the run; worth knowing if you ever have to make a quick exit.' I was beginning to think it might be a good idea if we made a quick exit there and then. 'Don't worry,' he continued 'they'll like you all right, especially if you're a friend of mine.' I began to feel very friendly towards the professor. As we entered the home of Vera I found her to be a middle-aged buxom woman, very friendly and kind. She had a tall thin husband whom I will call Charlie, and numerous children of different ages crawling over the floor and furniture. The appearance of the professor threw the whole family into pure ecstasy; it was clear to me that they thought the world of him. The best tea cups having been brought out, logs were thrown on the fire and as if by magic food appeared on the table. If rough and ready, these people were also kind, as the professor pointed out, the salt of the earth. Charlie suggested that Cullen must go and see 'the boys'. To this the professor needed no second bidding; so with a promise that we would bring Charlie safely back afterwards we took our temporary farewell of Vera.

Obviously the professor knew the district well as his car took us round bends, down dismal streets. Here and there strange groups gathered talking on the ill lit corners; I could well imagine that if one looked for trouble one would soon find it in this area. Soon the car pulled up outside a pub; the professor, Charlie and I, entered. If the pub appeared bleak on the outside it was certainly packed and lively on the inside. I was amazed at the reception that Professor Cullen received. Everyone seemed to know him and welcome him with open arms. It seemed impossible for me to buy a round of drinks, and more than I dared to refuse one. We had soon gathered a strange collection of friends: a Dutchman with whom we conversed in German (for we both spoke that language after a fashion); two tough looking seamen and a few other types. The pub we visited had microphones for Saturday night turns which seemed to be popular in Dockland. The professor needless to say soon took over the microphone, making himself compere, singer and comedian; all of which he excelled at, to the great pleasure of the audience. I pointed out that we had agreed to turn up at certain clubs that night; but each time he remembered one more pub we must visit to see some old friends. Eventually I gave up hope and regret to state that we failed to make the promised appearances at any of the clubs. But what we lost by not visiting London's West End, we made up for by seeing Dockland by night. At last having quenched our thirsts at heaven knows how many inns, having also met many more of the professor's friends (apparently ninety nine per cent of Dockland) it was time to go. A large crate of beer was bought by Cullen and placed in the car, bottles heaped in the coffin on the roof, and he drove us all back to Vera's house where an excellent spread was laid out for us on her table.

In the early hours of the morning, at about six o'clock, we said farewell to Vera, Charlie and everyone promising to return again one day, and drove off. So Sunday morning found us leaving London once again for the beauty and peace of the Sussex countryside. Some papers claimed that I did the return journey still lying in the coffin. But I can assure you that this is not so. I was well wrapped up sitting in the front seat next to the driver. So the rattling sound that came from the top of the van was not my teeth chattering in the cold morning air, but rather a few crates of empty beer bottles which we had dumped in my coffin on top of the van and which were swaying and rattling to the somewhat spasmodic rhythm of the professor's early morning driving. Several newspapers covered the story. One of the best was the following:-

Hastings Stuntman's Endurance Drive

THE GREAT OMANI, yoga expert and stuntman, last weekend successfully attempted his biggest ever personal endurance test when he made a journey to London stripped to the waist despite the bitter cold, sitting on top of a van driven by Professor Cullen, the palmist, in a coffin sprinkled with broken glass. Omani told an Observer reporter this week that the journey was very rough going and several times he felt that after another few miles he would have lost consciousness; the broken glass gave him no trouble at all. On arrival in London, Omani was just given time to thaw out before being whisked off to the BBC's *In Town Tonight* studio. Whilst in the studio Professor Cullen seized the opportunity to read the palm of Miiko Tako the lovely Japanese star of the new Marlon Brando film *Sayonara*. While driving through London the professor distributed three hundred and fifty 'Visit Hastings' publicity pamphlets to passers by.

Omani said that he has felt no after effects from their journey. As for Professor Cullen, he is at present in bed recovering from a severe cold!

THE CONCRETE
BLOCK

AH, OMANI,' BOOMED the earpiece of the telephone, 'why haven't you been in touch sooner?' I apologised to the professor and told him that I'd been looking for work. 'Work?' boomed the professor, in a horrified voice. 'My dear Omani, only fools and donkeys work. You appear to be a cross between the two. My dear chap, a stuntman of your capabilities, look at the amazing things you have done. You should be in films all the time, you should be working all the time. Your trouble is you are a damn bad businessman. You need my guidance.' The professor's salvo having been delivered, I waited for him to pause. 'Well, that's what I'm phoning about. I have an idea for a new stunt, a good one.' 'Splendid,' boomed the professor, 'I'll pick you up in half an hour.' He was as good as his word.

A little later on in the morning, the professor's car pulled up outside a public house. In a matter of minutes I was being shepherded in through the saloon bar door. 'You will like the landlord here,' confided the professor. 'A good fellow, we were in India together.' It is surprising the number of people who seem to have been in India at the same time as Cullen. For a change, the introductions were quickly over. Usually, when he introduces me it is like a ringmaster introducing the next act at some circus. It goes something like this:

'This is Omani. You know, the famous escapologist (usually they don't). You must have seen him do his daring dives into fire. You should have seen him when he rode the Wall of Death in a straitjacket, and there was the time when he was buried alive in a coffin

28

and nearly didn't come up. Gamest boy in the country.' By this time everybody is edging a little nearer towards us, hoping to find out whether this is true or whether we are a pair of lunatics. 'Omani,' continues the professor, 'show them how to eat glass.' At this stage a worried look begins to spread over the landlord's face as he sees his glasses being greedily eyed by me. By this time it is safe to say that a small and interested audience have openly gathered around us, and everybody wants to now be in on the act. Somebody calls for a round of drinks for the professor and myself, and this, I have no doubt, is exactly what the professor had in mind in the first place.

Eventually, the professor and I became seated at a table. 'Now Omani, what is this latest idea of yours? Have a drink first and take your time.' We lifted our glasses and drank to our mutual health. 'Professor,' I said, feeling fortified with my swig of Guinness, 'you are looking at the world's first Living Human Fossil.' 'You don't look that old,' commented the professor. Ignoring the wisecrack, I continued: 'This is the stunt as I see it, but I have not worked out all the details yet. I am going to be entombed inside a ton block of concrete, my whole body up to the neck, only my head will be free. Then I shall travel like this in the block of concrete on top of a lorry from Hastings to Piccadilly Circus. Same route as before, when we did the coffin trip.' The professor remained silent for a bit, stroking his head, then he called for two more drinks, and repeating my words, he said slowly, 'Entombed inside a block of concrete, only your head showing.' There was another pause, then he burst out, 'Excellent, Omani. Excellent. Perfect follow-up to our last stunt. Only one

29

thing worries me. How the hell can you do it? Apart from any other difficulties that may crop up, you realise I suppose that concrete expands when it sets. You would be crushed. So tell me: how do you propose to do it? Just tell me that.' Blowing out my chest and feeling pleased with myself, (this feeling of satisfaction was no doubt due to the Guinness I had had and to the fact that at last I had my old friend the professor guessing) I said: 'This is how I propose to do it.' Slowly and at some length I laid my plans before him. Eventually at the end he looked pleased. 'Excellent, my dear Omani, excellent. I will get in touch with the press right away. We will try and sell the exclusive story to one of the nationals and we will also contact the BBC. My dear Omani, we must drink to our new adventure: "The Concrete Block Stunt." No, no, drinks on me, I insist, finish that one first.' I did, and in no time at all another round had been set in front of us.

'Now,' said Cullen, 'who is going to put you into the block, who will do the work?' 'I know two good chaps on the building site,' I retorted. 'They know all about concrete work. They are just the right lads for the job.' 'This will be quite a stunt,' said Cullen. 'Anyway, that's all we can do for the moment.' We gathered our things together then bade farewell to the landlord. The first part of our plans had been set. I was to get the cement and contact the two chaps I had in mind, Bert and Tom. The professor, for his part, would handle the publicity and contact the newspapers, and our friends at the BBC. We took temporary leave of each other and went our separate ways.

My next meeting with Cullen showed that he had not been wasting his time. One of the well-known Sunday newspapers had agreed to cover the story. He had also got the BBC Outside Broadcasting Unit interested: they too were going to cover it. 'We will take more or less the same route as before,' announced the professor. 'On the way we will stop at Sevenoaks and let the Kent papers take some pictures. A pal of mine has a pub in Sevenoaks and we will call in there: an excellent place for publicity.' The last part I heard with mixed feelings. I had visions of the professor and the reporters enjoying themselves in the pub while I remained outside, stuck in my block on the lorry. It had been arranged that film actor Andrew Faulds would interview me for the BBC at Sevenoaks.

Eventually the morning of the big event arrived, and the first reporter on the scene was from the Sunday newspaper. By the time he arrived I had already been entombed in the middle of the big block of concrete, which weighed about one ton. The block was, of course, already on the lorry ready for our journey. Yes, there was I at last completely covered in a ton of concrete; only my head remained outside. If my body was unable to move, at least I could move my head a few inches. The Sunday newspaper reporter examined the block slowly and with suspicion, but eventually he was satisfied that I was well and truly in it.

The procession which was to head for Piccadilly Circus was to be as follows: first Professor Pat Cullen, ex-regimental sergeant-major, would lead the way with his streamer-covered car, red beard and long flowing hair. Second came the lorry containing the concrete block with me stuck in it. On the lorry with me were Bert and Tom standing by with fourteen-pound hammers at the ready. Sitting behind me on the lorry was a nurse, and a pretty one: I chose her personally. Following behind us in his car would be the Sunday newspaper reporter, suspiciously watching every move. He intended to follow us the whole way, and he did. The lorry had been kindly lent to us by a lady, Mrs Lane, who lived in Hastings. A very charming person.

The hour for our departure was to be 10.30 am. The professor had worked out a carefully planned timetable and had every intention that it should be stuck to with precision. The professor, who basically was a very military character, was determined that everybody must be ready at 10.30 sharp. There was much synchronising of watches among those who could afford them. An early morning crowd had gathered at the old town, Hastings, to see us off, and to get some interesting pictures. With two minutes to zero hour, at last the time for departure had nearly arrived. The large bulk of Professor Cullen took his place at the head of the procession. 'Are we ready?' he shouted, glancing at his watch. 'Thirty seconds to go... ten seconds... Everybody FORWARD.' The professor waved his arms, giving the impression that he was ordering a bayonet charge, leapt into his car and shot forward, leading the procession. The crowd gave a good-natured cheer. For our part, our lorry engine roared up, backfired twice and stopped. In fact, it never started. Out jumped our driver and started to crank the lorry hard. Except for a few spluttering sounds and a good deal of smoke, nothing happened. In the meantime, the professor, blissfully ignorant of what was happening, or rather what was not happening, sailed on and out of sight in the firm belief that he was in his rightful place leading the procession and that we lesser mortals were behind him, as indeed we should have been. Having seen the advance publicity in connection with this stunt, quite a few people lined the first part of the route to see us go by. Little wonder then that they looked at each other, rather puzzled, when all they saw was the professor bowing and waving to them in the firm belief that the much publicised procession was right behind him. It has been said that his actions looked rather like those of Her Majesty the Queen when waving and smiling to the crowds before entering Buckingham Palace. In the meantime, my driver was cranking the lorry as hard as he could go, and talking to it not so quietly under his breath. By this time, the Sunday newspaper reporter was making helpful suggestions to the driver, as were some of the crowd who now found the lorry engine more interesting than me. The nurse was sitting beside me shivering and I was lying helpless in the middle of a ton block of concrete. Blissfully ignorant of all that was happening, the professor still sailed on in his car until he looked behind him and saw that he was the only one in the procession. In the meantime the lorry driver cranked away and mopped his brow and swore a thousand curses. The nurse continued to shiver and give me numerous black looks. The Sunday newspaper reporter chewed his pencil and I still lay embedded in my concrete.

Needless to say, it was not long before the professor's car swung round again and headed back to the starting point to see what had happened to us. Suddenly, he arrived back on the scene, not in the best of moods. 'What's wrong?' he thundered. 'Why isn't the lorry working?' 'Don't know,' said the driver, 'it was working perfectly yesterday. In fact we went for a ride in her, practically out all day we was. Took the kids out we did, and as grandma was down...' 'Never mind your family history,' roared the professor, 'have you checked the petrol?' The driver called to one of his mates. 'You filled her up this morning, didn't you, Jim?' 'No,' retorted Jim, 'I thought you were going to do it.' 'Then fill her up, man,' roared the infuriated professor, 'we are already thirteen and a quarter minutes late.' The professor was heard to mumble something about how he would like to have that lot under him in the army. It is surprising the difference petrol will make to a lorry, and it was surprising the difference the professor made to the drive: both were going in double-quick time.

The lorry was soon in working order and for the second time the professor waved his arms dramatically, shouted '...FORWARD...' and leapt into his car. Our lorry engine revved up, and at a slow pace we rolled forward with Cullen once again at the head of the procession. The procession had now started. Following us with his eyes firmly fixed on the block came the Sunday newspaper reporter. The procession, though late, was now well and truly on its way. Except for the cement dust which kept blowing in my eyes despite the fact that I was wearing goggles, the journey turned out to be more comfortable than my previous one when I travelled in a coffin along much the same route. The whole procession was now travelling at a fairly steady pace. The professor however, occasionally left the front of the procession and shot ahead out of sight, a sort of advance scouting party to warn people that we were on our way.

At a given signal from the professor the procession came to a halt outside a pub at Sevenoaks. Cullen thought that the Sunday newspaper reporter might like to take a picture of me being given a drink. The reporter was all for this and could see no reason why he shouldn't have one himself. As I was lying flat with nearly a ton of concrete on top of me, and as I was not able to move my head much, how was I going to be able to drink? My nurse, who had spent much of the journey shivering on top of the lorry and giving me black looks, came up with a good idea. 'Insert the funnel into his mouth,' she said, 'then pour the liquid into the funnel. In that position there's just a chance it might choke him!'

A suitable funnel was found by the landlord and was duly stuck in my mouth. A fair measure of rum was then poured into the funnel and trickled down into my stomach, all of which made me cough and splutter. The newspaper reporter enjoyed this little scene and took quite a few pictures of it. It was soon time to start our journey towards London again, so after a farewell to the landlord and the small bemused crowd who had gathered round us, once again the procession started to roll, led of course by the vast form of the professor. Our next appointment en route was to meet Andrew Faulds who was going to interview us for the BBC Outside Broadcast Unit.

By now the nurse, who had helped us to find the bottle of rum and who no doubt had also helped herself to it, had stopped shivering and begun to look upon me with much more favour. As has already been stated we were running very late and Andrew Faulds, who had been waiting for us to turn up for some considerable time, was just about to give up and return to London when we came puffing round the corner. Explanations over, it was time for him to board the lorry for the interview. This would be tape-recorded then rushed back to London to be edited in time for the evening programme.

I have been interviewed by the BBC in many ways over the years, including hanging upside down in a straitjacket and standing on my head on the extreme edge of Beachy Head. This interview proved to be the most uncomfortable one of the lot, as sand and cement dust kept clogging my nostrils and getting into my eyes, in spite of the fact that I was wearing goggles.

Both the professor and I were interviewed. Frankly, I cannot re-member much about the interview or the questions that he asked. One question however I do remember. 'Omani,' he said, 'you are entombed in concrete. What do you do if you get taken short?' In those far-off days when the BBC led the world in respectability, that was quite a question. I forget what my reply was but I believe it was suitable. Of course the old stunt of eating light bulbs had to come into it again. The professor, much to the delight of the cameramen, fed me with bits of Osram electric light bulb. The sound effect of chewing glass over the mike is terrific and it promptly set my nurse shivering again and got me some more black looks. The interview having finally been recorded and Andrew Faulds and the professor having had some eats and drinks, and I having had a throatful of glass and an eyeful of cement dust, we were ready to start rolling again towards the unsuspecting London.

The rest of the journey was really uneventful for me. I just lay in my block watching rows of chimneys and rooftops glide past me, until finally Piccadilly hove into sight and once again we took it in our stride. It had much the same psychological effect on the Piccadilly crowds as the time before when I circled round the ever-youthful Eros in my coffin. In fact, Eros was the only one who was not affected by it. Little wonder, for this sender of love-shafts has been watching cranks go past for the best part of his nymphlike little life and like myself, nothing ever surprises him any more. However, the flesh-and-bone public reacted in various ways. Certainly they had never seen anybody in concrete before. One lady pointing frantically with her umbrella was of the opinion that the young man should be put away for his own safety. Many no doubt were of that opinion. But one thing was certain: never before had they seen a living person entombed in concrete. Equally certain is the fact that as far as I am concerned they will never see it again.

Eventually, having completed the journey, it was time for me to get out of the ton of concrete, unseen of course by the public. By now, let me assure you, I had had enough. We drove into a big yard and the gates closed behind us. For the public the show was over. Actually, in some ways now the hard part started. You see it was now time for me to be removed from the block, and if anyone here is a palaeontologist then you will know just how hard it is to remove a fossil from a stone. I'm not telling you how I escaped from my ton block of concrete. It still to many remains a mystery, but eventually I was out. It took me quite a few minutes to control my balance; it took me quite a little time before I could walk. For a time I swayed like a drunken man. Soon my circulation improved and once again all became normal.

Margaret Cullen, the professor's wife has up to now been mentioned very little if at all. Margaret, a friend of mine for many years, is a brilliant clairvoyant. There are many people from the four corners of the earth who seek her advice. At the moment of writing she has probably had more radio interviews and television appearances than I've had, which is saying something. The difference between Margaret and myself is that she is famous but very modest and never talks about her fame. Me, I never stop.

It was to Margaret's place in London that we went. With me were my nurse, Tom and Bert and of course the professor. As always, Margaret had a warm greeting for us all and soon was plying us with hot cups of excellent tea and cakes. In this friendly and peaceful atmosphere, even my nurse, whom it will be remembered had spent a lot of the journey giving me black looks, beamed upon me with the utmost benevolence. Those cups of tea were some of the best I can remember, as they washed the cement dust down my throat.

Many years have passed since this stunt was performed. Margaret practises her clairvoyance in Brighton now. She still possesses a smile that dwarfs that of the Mona Lisa, she still has the wisdom of Omar Khayam and she still makes a damn good cup of tea.

That evening we all listened to the radio to hear our interviews, and they were not at all bad. As I had been paid by the BBC and the newspapers for concrete services rendered it was my duty as a good citizen, and still my duty if I wasn't, to report my takings to the Ministry of Labour on my return to Hastings. So, like a good citizen I headed for the labour exchange and like many good citizens found myself at a depressing-looking counter. 'Name,' said the man. I told him. 'You're seeking employment here?' 'No, I have come to declare some takings.' 'Who were you working for?' 'Self-employed.' 'Doing what?' 'Travelling in concrete.' 'You own a cement works?' 'No,' I said. 'What I mean is I was not exactly travelling in concrete trying to sell it. No, I was just travelling in concrete, like a sort of human fossil. That's it. I was entombed in a block of concrete like a sort of human fossil, and like this I travelled to Piccadilly Circus.'

The counter clerk looked at me in a strange way, then hastily whispered into the ear of a second man. The second man gave me a quick glance then found it necessary to whisper into the ear of a third man. The third man found it necessary to hasten to a door marked 'Manager'. And I found it necessary to bolt for a door marked EXIT…

WALL OF
DEATH

I FOUND MYSELF staring into the eyes of a large, unfriendly Alsatian wolfhound, whose look told me in no uncertain manner that I had no right to be where I was. The mat he stood upon did not have 'Welcome' written on it. We both knew that the moment I made a move he would make a grab at me.

I lifted a stern and slightly trembling finger and stared back at him. This, however, neither impressed nor fooled the dog in the slightest. A change of tactics was needed. I decided to try my own particular brand of diplomacy on the infuriated hound. I called him all sorts of nice doggie names, such as 'Prince' and 'Flash'; I even promoted him to 'Rex'. But flattery was getting me nowhere, which made me think it must be a male dog. What I have found sometimes works on widows, does not appear to work on Alsatians!

This impossible situation of the pair of us staring at each other might have continued for ages, but for a gruff voice that suddenly called out, 'What you want, mister?' 'I want,' I replied, 'you to call this animal off. If we can accomplish this feat without the loss of too many limbs, then I should like to see the owner of this establishment.' 'What's yer name?' repeated the voice, suspiciously. 'I am,' I said, pulling myself up to my full five feet eight inches, 'THE GREAT OMANI.' At that moment, however, I felt particularly small. 'Oh.' said the voice, 'So you're the Great Omani.' At least he seemed to know my name. 'One moment, guv. I'll see the boss.' He gave a whistle and the dog slunk away, not without a disappointed and lingering look at the seat of my pants.

42

Eventually I was ushered into a caravan, where a young man held out his hand. 'Come right in, Mr Omani.' He spoke with a slight American accent which may, or may not, have been put on. This, then, was the boss of the famous MGM Wall of Death team. 'Sorry about the dog; gotta have one on fairgrounds, never know who's prowling around. Now, what can I do for you?' 'I am wondering if we could work a publicity stunt together on the Wall of Death,' I ventured. 'I'd like to very much,' he said, 'but what? Practically everything has been done on it already.' 'Supposing,' I said, 'I travelled round whilst strapped in a straitjacket. Has that ever been done before?'

He thought for a few seconds and replied, 'No, no, it hasn't; by heck, you've got an idea there.' 'Could it be done?' I enquired doubtfully. 'Because, to tell you the truth, I've never even seen a Wall of Death.' 'Why, yes, I reckon it could. You would have to be placed in the straitjacket, then lifted onto the handlebars and then you would have to lean well back. I would drive you round myself. Of course, we'd need a letter covering us in case of accident, but that's only a matter of form. Yes,' he continued, 'that will draw the public; it's never been done before.' 'Splendid,' I said, though I am not sure that I felt it. 'But I must have a few practice runs first.' 'Of course,' he agreed. 'Come round tomorrow afternoon at about three o'clock, then we will have a try-out. If you're happy with it, we will pull this stunt off on Saturday evening as it's the last night of the fair.' We shook hands and agreed to meet on the morrow at 3pm.

I then informed the press that on the following Saturday I would attempt a 'World Premiere' stunt (I thought 'World Premiere' sounded good) which would be to ride round the Wall of Death in a straitjacket. This, then, was the gimmick: I would have to sit on the motorbike without being able to hold on.

That afternoon I arrived home in time for tea. 'You're looking pleased with yourself,' said Marvita, 'what are you up to now?' 'Do I have to be up to anything? Well, as a matter of fact, I'm going to do another stunt.' 'I know,' said Marvita, 'you're going to jump off Beachy Head with an umbrella for a parachute.' 'Nothing of the sort,' I said indignantly, 'I'm going to ride the Wall of Death in a straitjacket. It has never been done before.' 'You see, I was right,' said Marvita. 'I always said you'd end up in a straitjacket.' 'You can laugh, but wait until you see the crowds flock to this one.' 'I wonder,' said Marvita, 'what it would be like to be married to a normal person?' 'Terrible,' I replied; and poured myself out another cup of tea.

The next day I kept my appointment and three o'clock found me standing in the pit of the Wall of Death looking up rather nervously at the giant perpendicular walls. My young American friend who owned the outfit was there to meet me. 'Now,' he said, 'once you're sitting on the handlebars, all you have to do is to lean well back onto me.' This sounded simple enough. 'Shall we try it first without the straitjacket?' I suggested. 'Just to get the feel of it.' 'Don't worry,

44

you won't feel much!' said the grinning mechanic, who was standing close by. This remark didn't altogether put me at my ease.

I was lifted in a sitting position onto the handlebars of the bike and, carrying out instructions, leant well back onto the chest of my driver. He, in turn, locked his jaw over my shoulder, holding me in position. The time had come for my first spin on the Wall of Death. I was wondering whether it might also be my last...

We started to circle round the bottom of the pit. Then, suddenly, the engine roared and the next thing I knew was that we were flying through the air at what appeared a terrific speed and at a most unusual angle. Everything seemed to whizz past upside down. The mechanics who had lifted me on were standing at the bottom of the pit (which, to me, seemed a long way beneath me now) looking up at me with foolish grins upon their equally foolish faces. Omani, stuntman, escapologist and what have you was now giving his famous impersonation of a neurotic angel exceeding the speed limit in outer space. Indeed, the way things were going, I was beginning to think that the impersonation of an angel would soon become the reality. By looking in front of me I became very giddy, but soon remedied this by looking straight above me; this way I did not see the scenery flash past. Suddenly, my driver shouted 'We're going down.' And then it happened. I felt myself falling down and down, more rapidly every second. My heart seemed to leap into my mouth and the next thing I knew we were gliding round the bottom of the pit, just as we had started. The grinning mechanics lifted me off the handlebars, but my feet swayed under me a bit as once again I stood on terra firma. 'You'll find it easier next time,' said the driver, and my second trip, this time with the straitjacket on, was successful. I was now quite happy about the whole thing, except the coming down to land part. This is the most difficult part to get used to: that horrible feeling that you are falling. But after a few more practice runs I had got more used to it and was quite ready to present the stunt on the following evening in front of the press and public.

Eventually, the Saturday morning arrived and the local papers carried the advance publicity to the effect that '... this evening Omani will attempt his daring ride on the Wall of Death at 7pm. A stunt that no one [and this was quite true] has ever done before in a straitjacket.'

That evening, Marvita and I, and a few friends, including Professor Cullen, found ourselves entering the fairground. Like all fairs, we were met with flashing lights, hurdy-gurdy music and that atmosphere which only a fair can produce. We passed a few side-shows, one of which was billed as 'Dora, The Rat Girl'. I had to have a sixpenny-worth of this, as the poster displayed a beautiful girl surrounded by large and fierce-looking rats. The scene inside was rather different to the exciting-looking poster outside. Dora was there alright, lying in a cage, clad in a bikini – and she was knitting! A few rather over-fed and rather sleepy white rats, who were obviously bored with the whole show, huddled together in a corner. Rather an anti-climax, but never mind – Dora's bikini was worth the tanner! We left Dora and her rodent friends and continued on our way.

Soon the well lit-up Wall of Death came into sight and a large crowd was standing outside watching a girl and man sitting on motorbikes, revving up their engines, whilst the crowd excitedly pressed closer. Nearby a man stood on a platform, holding a microphone in his hand and telling the crowd about the thrills and spills of the Wall of Death. Suddenly, he spotted me making my way towards him. He pointed dramatically in my direction as he shouted 'And here he comes, Ladies and Gentlemen, the man you have been waiting for, your own local star, the man who is here once again to defy death; a big hand for Mr Omani!' He had put everything into this little spiel and, with a last burst of admiration for Mr Omani, he flung his arms into the air, lost his balance and fell off the platform! He was soon back on again, waving his arms and shouting. He drew the crowds in large numbers; he was an excellent and highly-skilled spieler. He made a few more flowery remarks about me, whilst Marvita nudged her companion, at the same time pointing at me. 'Look at him, lapping it all up,' she whispered, 'he's oozing with conceit.' 'And why not?' I retorted, 'After all, the man's quite right!' He beckoned me onto the platform. 'Here you are, my friends,' he continued, 'your own star – Mr Omani.' 'The Great Omani,' I hissed in his ear. 'The Great Omani,' repeated the man, 'is about to present a feat never before seen on the Wall – as advertised in today's papers, he will travel round the Wall in a straitjacket.'

Whilst this was going on, I suddenly spotted out of the corner of my eye, Professor Cullen surrounded by Teddy Boys and holding one of them – a weedy-looking specimen – up in the air by his coat collar. He had made some rude remark about me in the hearing of the professor, who now stood with his shoulder-length long hair and ginger beard blowing angrily in the breeze, while he waved his massive fist at the Teddies, challenging them to a fight. They took one look at his large and quivering form and wisely – and quickly – disappeared.

Meanwhile, the show was about to commence. The motorbike engines revved up. Marvita and an assistant were struggling to put me into the straitjacket; a restraint which is far harder to get into than get out of! Eventually, after a lot of heaving and pulling, the jacket was on, the buckles and tapes were done up and I was ready for the journey. The place was packed out and the sign 'Full House' went up. The motorbikes drove down the ramp into the pit of the Wall of Death. I followed, a big door closed behind us and we were sealed inside the pit.

The crowds were all at the top of the Wall, guarded by a safety-rail, just in case a bike should shoot over the top. A mass of faces were peering down at us, eagerly watching every move of our preparations. I was lifted onto the motorbike handlebars. Once again, I leant well back and felt my driver hook his jaw over my shoulder. The cameramen were flashing away, taking pictures. We were ready now for the show.

The engine roared and once again I found myself flying round the Wall of Death. The faces of the audience flashed past me ... round and round the circular wall we went, climbing higher and higher. My memory was suddenly jerked back over the bridge of years. It reminded my of my first flight in an aeroplane. At that time I was a junior boy at Sherborne School in Dorset. An air circus was visiting nearby. I paid ten shillings and six pence for a flight which included 'looping the loop'. Why the craft never fell to pieces during this manoeuvre is a mystery. At last we were flashing round the top of the Wall of Death, mighty close to the safety-rail, I thought.

But, as it happened, I was enjoying it thoroughly. Eventually, it was time to come down again and I got myself ready for the falling feeling. This time I seemed to be more used to it and once again we found ourselves – I'm glad to say in one piece – circling round the bottom of the pit.

Frankly, I was amazed at the applause that greeted us. People were cheering and clapping. I was lifted off the handlebars onto the ground. As my feet touched the ground I swayed and staggered, and as I fell forward I was caught just in time by one of the mechanics. This part, I must confess, was pre-arranged. In fact, I could have walked as well as anybody there, unlike Professor Cullen who, having discovered the fairground bar, was rapidly approaching the stage where he could not walk at all. My unsteady gait brought forth cheers and more applause – and there, my friends, you have a perfect example of cunning mixed with good showmanship.

The next thing I knew, something whizzed past my head, landing at my feet. It was a penny. Then started the most fantastic and certainly the most pleasant rainstorm I've ever witnessed. Pennies, sixpenny pieces, half-a-crowns, the lot; all came showering down into the pit. The crowds were actually throwing money at us. The whole show had been a big success and, from a financial point of view, certainly 'Pennies from Heaven'.

There was still a large crowd outside, disappointed because they couldn't get in. In the end I performed about six times; in fact, I went on non-stop until the fair closed at midnight. Rather sadly, I shook hands with my friends of the famous MGM Wall of Death and bade them farewell. When I left, the carnival lights had all been extinguished. A dark velvet sky studded with tiny twinkling stars peacefully lit the way home. A cool breeze gently blew in from the sea, blowing away the dust and fumes.

I was just about to leave the Carnival ground when something loomed up in front of me stopping me dead in my tracks. It was a large fierce-looking hound. My heart missed a beat; we had met before. Suddenly, it rubbed its huge head up against my body, gave me a friendly wag of its tail as if to say goodbye, and then disappeared as silently as it had come, into the darkness of the night.

The following appeared in one of the newspapers:

Round 'Wall Of Death' In Straitjacket

Nearly everyone celebrated the last night of the Carnival week in one way or another. Easily the most original and the most daring was that of the Great Omani, escapologist at Hastings Pier. First he allowed himself to be strapped into a straitjacket with his arms pinned behind his back. He was then lifted onto the handlebars of the motorcycle and driven around the 'Wall of Death'. One of the main attractions of the Carnival Fair.

This, it was claimed, was the first time that a feat of this nature had ever been performed. And so many people wished to see it that the Great Omani was driven around six times by the MGM riders instead of the scheduled once, and the show continued non-stop until the Fair closed...

THE BURNING
HOUSE

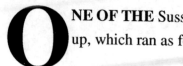 NE OF THE Sussex newspapers gave me a small write-up, which ran as follows:

> Passers-by who see a man in a straitjacket hanging up-side down from the top of Christ Church, St. Leonard's School Buildings, at three o'clock this afternoon need not be unduly alarmed. It will be the daring film and TV stuntman, The Great Omani, in another shot for the GIB Film (Hastings) Ltd., new production, *Dare Devils at Play.* The Great Omani, who had a narrow escape a fortnight ago in the "Burning House" scene for the same film, which is directed by Mr G. Ivan Barnett, states that his exploit this afternoon takes place during the Christ Church school midsummer fair and that those present are likely to be filmed for crowd scenes.

Yes, I remember the blazing house stunt well, in fact I'm never likely to forget it. Let me tell you about it.

The flames licked over my clothed body then retreated for a few seconds only to return again with renewed vigour. The walls of the little room were now blazing. Yellow flames seemed to be shooting and darting everywhere. Part of the cardboard and straw roof fell to the ground with a crash, sending up a shower of sparks and smoke… the heat was becoming stifling. I lay with my face pressed tightly to the ground. The small room was now a blazing inferno, inside as well as out. An icy cold fear crept over my body because I knew that any minute now the rest of the roof would cave in. With every nerve alert I waited for the sound of the motorbike which we had planned would crash through the blazing cardboard walls. The seconds seemed like hours until I heard the engine approaching. Then, suddenly with a roar, the motorbike crashed into the blazing house, right through the flaming cardboard walls and out the other side, on fire. The first shots and sound recordings of the planned all-action GIB film, *Dare Devils at Play* had been taken. It was now my cue to bolt out through the gap torn in the wall by the motorbike, but the petrol had been sprayed far too heavily over the whole place, and so the hole I should have bolted through was a mass of flame. The house was, in fact, a solid block of fire... I had not enough room to get up sufficient speed to carry me through. However, with the roof likely to cave in at any second, I needed no second bidding. I rushed for the gap with all the speed I could muster, covered my face with my hands and plunged into – and through – the flames. I felt the full force of the soaring flames lick my hands. Blindly, I half-rushed, half-fell through this inferno. I don't quite know how, but I got through the wall of fire and staggered choking into the fresh air. As I collapsed onto the ground I saw the rest of the straw roof of our petrol soaked house fall to the ground. It had missed me by seconds...

The back of both my hands had been burnt. In a matter of seconds the St. John's Ambulance man was bending over me, dressing my burns. Soon an ambulance arrived and I was placed into it. Marvita got in beside me. As the ambulance bell rang the crowd moved back and gave me a cheer. This didn't do much to stop the pain, but it did,

I suppose, do something to raise my deflated ego. We were on our way, once again if I may say so, to the Royal East Sussex County Hospital. All the time the cameras had been turning. This accident, of course, was not something we had counted on, and quite definitely it was, as they say, a turn up for the books.

Next day my hands came up like balloons, but thanks to the excellent care of the hospital, they were soon cured. Strange as it my seem, not even a scar is there to tell the tale.

My friend G Ivan Barnett, director of the GIB Film Company (Hastings) certainly got some good shots for his film, *Dare Devils at Play*, and if it should so happen one day I am sitting in a cinema and this film is being shown and some young man whispers knowingly into his girlfriend's ear: ''e don't really get burnt, luv, that's all fake camera work, that is' then so help me, I shall crown him.

BURIED
ALIVE IN A
MONASTERY
GARDEN

I FIRST SAW the monastery standing bleak and deserted against the dark and wintry sky. The wind was high and beat the rain against the hard stone walls, sending it trickling back onto the cobblestone streets and eventually winding its way into the waiting tumultuous sea. The monastery had long been deserted by the monks, and the grounds and buildings were now used for exhibitions and for the social life of the inhabitants of the small Sussex town called Rye. Anybody who has ever visited this little town will know of its ancient beauty. They will remember the cobblestone streets, the ancient buildings and many other things of interest. Yes, this place, like so many of the towns and villages of Sussex, is well worth a visit.

There are still those to be found who will sit in the corner of some ancient pub and tell you tales of the past: of smugglers who crossed the marshes at night, whose footsteps were muffled by the moaning wind and the cry of the night birds; of footpads who lurked in dark and narrow passages; of the hidden rooms and trapdoors which some say can still be found in the timber-beamed houses. It was business, however, which brought me to Rye. A trades exhibition was to be held in the disused monastery and Marvita and I had been booked as an attraction to help draw in the people. Whilst discussing the exhibition many were the tales told about this ancient monastery building. One story in particular is worth retelling, for it is based on fact. The story went something like this…

One afternoon a young monk was taking a stroll in the monastery gardens. As he went on his way, no doubt in deep meditation, a ball came hurtling over the monastery wall and landed at his feet. Surprised, the monk looked up to find out the cause of this strange happening, and as he did so a young girl popped her head over the wall and asked for the ball to be thrown back. As the story was told to me, she was very beautiful, and I quite believe it. The ball having landed by mistake in the grounds, the young monk, who by now had got over his surprise, picked it up and, no doubt with much flowing of robes, sent it hurtling back over the wall. And so they went their separate ways. This, however, was not to be the end of their meetings but, as you will see, the beginning, because most afternoons when the monk took his stroll in the gardens the good old ball came hurtling over the top. Yes, eventually and inevitably it had to happen: the young pair fell in love. Now this was a very naughty thing for him to do; as no doubt his brother monks pointed out to him, the better monks do not go around falling in love with strange young women. However, there is no doubt in my mind that this one was a particularly intelligent young monk.

One night, as a cloud passed over the moon, he crept out of his cell, scrambled over the monastery wall – which up to now appears to have been used as an ecclesiastical tennis net – and finding the girl waiting for him on the other side, they did just what I would have done: wisely ran for their blessed lives. The young couple, having eloped, headed for the Sussex coastline and I think they got as far as one of my favourite beauty spots near Hastings, called Fairlight Glen.

Incidentally, if you have never been to Fairlight Glen and you find yourself in the Hastings area, make a point of walking along the cliffs from Hastings to this beauty spot: it's quite a long walk but well worth it. I never tire of its beauty.

Although I have made light of this story up to now, it ends in a most horrible way. The monks pursued the young couple, and at Fairlight Glen caught up with them. A battle of swords ensued but the monk was outnumbered and during the battle had his arm cut off. He was dragged back to the monastery and promptly buried alive. There are those who claim to see his ghost walk at Rye monastery. It is said by some that he is still searching for the young girl.

Now this is where I come back into the picture because, as I mentioned before, Marvita and I were booked to appear as an attraction at an exhibition to be held in the monastery. The feat that I was to perform was that of being buried alive in a coffin, a stunt which never fails to draw the morbid. A marquee, large enough to hold an audience, was set up in the monastery grounds and it was here that I was to present the stunt. The committee had gone to the trouble of obtaining an elderly man, known as Henry, to assist me and it would not surprise me if at times people called him other names as well. One quickly discovered that Henry was the talkative type, although on occasions nobody knew what he was talking about; for that matter he probably didn't know himself.

On being introduced to Henry, he informed me that he had an extensive knowledge when it came to burying people, and in his day, as he put it, 'buried many a good 'un.' As the reporters and cameramen were to be present at my stunt, he seemed thrilled at the prospect of burying me. Indeed, he pointed out, 'When I buries 'em I make a good job on it and they don't come up again.' As I had every intention of coming up again I thought it was time I had a little heart-to-heart talk with Henry, and told him that irrespective of what his past clients did it was most certainly my intention to 'rise again'. 'But just suppose you don't,' persisted Henry with a look of happy anticipation on his countenance. 'Let us suppose nothing of the sort,' I said. 'If you follow my instructions carefully, all will be well. When you cover the coffin over with that vast pile of sand over there, put it on quickly but lightly. On no account trample it down or bang it down with your shovel. The coffin has no lid on so the weight of the sand will be directly on me; and believe me, the weight will be terrific. Marvita will be on the stage all the time with you...' 'As a matter of fact,' confided Henry suddenly, 'I whistles.' 'You what?' I asked. 'Whistles. You know, bird noises and the like... now, if you would like me to do a turn on the stage afore you gets in the coffin?' 'Well, no thank you, Henry,' I added hastily, 'I don't think bird noises will quite fit in with this type of show, although I'm sure your turn is very good.' 'I also recites,' persisted Henry, determined not to be done out of his big moment on the stage. 'They do say as 'ow I've got a gift for theatricals.' I refrained from asking who said so. Our conversation on the subject of Henry's undiscovered talents was, thank heavens, interrupted by the arrival of the committee's chairman, who quickly put a damper on the future of Henry's brilliant stage career. 'Are you quite satisfied with the arrangements, Mr Omani?' asked the chairman. 'Perfectly, thank you,' I replied. 'And does Henry know what is expected of him?' 'I know how to bury him governor, but I ain't never seen one come up afore; it ain't natural,' he continued, shaking his head.

I entered the coffin, sat upright, crossing my arms over my chest. Then my eyes closed and slowly the upper part of my body began to sway backwards and forwards. The whole place was now silent; nobody moved, the audience were staring fixedly at me. Suddenly the dramatic silence was broken by a croaky voice shouting, 'Are you ready now, guv?' Marvita hastily told Henry to keep quiet, or he would break my trance: an observation which brought forth a torrent of indecipherable words from Henry. Having now worked up sufficient tension among the audience, I sank slowly back into the coffin and was ready. Hastily, Marvita tucked a tarpaulin over my body – a protection to keep the sand out of my mouth, eyes and ears – but of course there was no lid to the coffin. Had there been, I would have had plenty of air to play with; and no crushing weight of sand direct on my body. I heard a woman in the front row say, 'He's in a trance alright: I've seen them before.' The audience heard her, luckily, and automatically believed her.

Suddenly I felt a thud and then another thud on top of me. Complete with the silver spade, Henry had started to bury me alive. It would take me a whole chapter to tell you how this is done. All I will say is that, in my opinion, being buried alive is one of the most difficult and terrifying of all stunts and certainly one of the most dangerous. The shovelling increased and the sand began to descend rapidly on me and the coffin. It soon seemed that the weight was becoming unusually heavy. My muscles were now tensed to take the strain: still the sand thudded over the coffin. There can't be much more, I thought, it seems like a ton already. But still the shovelfuls of sand descended. Henry was indeed working overtime, and his remark that 'when I buries 'em they don't come up again' began to make itself clear to me. I was now beginning to sweat; I had never had it as heavy as this before. There was a very small hole in the tarpaulin and through this some sand trickled down onto my face. Suddenly, with horror, I realised something had gone wrong. I broke into a sweat of fear and panic. The sand which had fallen onto my face was damp; if they put the full amount of sand on as arranged, I would be crushed to death, as with this stunt the sand must be bone-dry, otherwise the weight is far too great to withstand.

Frantically, I tried to struggle… but have you ever tried to move with a load of damp sand on top of you? It was impossible to move even a muscle. My arms, which were cradled over my head, were rapidly weakening with the weight; I couldn't hold it off much longer and if my arms gave in, the lot would cave in on top of me and I would be stifled. I now realised that there was little chance of escape; this time I had bitten off more than I could chew. I felt dizzy; my consciousness was beginning to slip away from me. I made a final effort to pull myself together and hold off the crushing weight.

I thought frantically of the outside world which I would never see again; I redoubled my efforts to hold off the disastrous moment. Suddenly it seemed to me that the thudding had stopped. I waited… was it my imagination, or was the load getting lighter? Desperately, I listened for a few agonising seconds; those seconds were the longest I can ever remember. But I was right: the load was getting lighter. they were digging me out.

As soon as it was possible to move, I did so, and my head popped up through the sand. I let fly with a vocabulary which I thought most fitting for the occasion; and of which, no doubt, even D. H. Lawrence would have approved.

Eventually, in my fear and rage, having blasphemed the committee, the monastery and in particular Henry, who stood there leaning on his silver shovel with his mouth open, I stumped off the stage, furious at the blunder but at the same time grateful to be alive. It had been a very near thing. Marvita, who has that peculiar thing known as woman's intuition, sensed that something was wrong, and just in time gave the order: 'Dig him out – quick!' I explained to the excited reporters that I had made a blunder of it because the sand was damp. The sand was promptly shovelled up into a boiler room to be dried in time for the next show. I, in turn, rushed round to the nearest bar and was glad to put some distance between the monastery and myself; and indeed everything associated with it.

I found myself a comfortable seat at the bar and was washing down some sand with an inviting-looking pint of beer when a voice bellowed in my ear, making me nearly spill the lot. 'Cor, guv, you gave me a turn up there; that you did.' I looked round, to see the ace of all shovellers, the Human Nightingale and Reciter of Recitations: Henry had found me. 'And you,' I said, removing my beer from his as quickly and as far as possible, 'gave *me* quite a turn! Have a drink, Henry.' 'I'll tell you something,' said Henry confidentially – it's surprising how confidential some people get on a pint of beer – 'I wouldn't have missed that for nothink; you were mighty near to joining that there monk they talks about.' 'Very,' I agreed. 'It's tempting the devil, being buried afore your time, and if that don't prove it, what do?' 'Nothing,' I said. 'Yer wants ter try yer 'and at whistling and reciting, like I does.' 'Yes,' I agreed. 'Mind you, I ain't saying you didn't do your best,' continued my companion, plonking his empty pint glass on the counter in front of me, which the landlord was not slow in refilling. 'But it just ain't natural to tempt the devil.' 'It ain't – I mean, it's not,' I agreed. At that point, the arrival of Marvita in the bar temporarily interrupted Henry's lecture. 'What are you having, Marvita?' I asked her. 'As if I didn't know. One whisky please, Landlord.' 'Hello missus,' said Henry with a broad grin, 'made a right charlie of 'imself tonight, didn't 'e?' 'And you can say that again,' said Marvita. 'Tonight he was the king of all charlies.'

Well, some years have passed since that night and I haven't seen Henry since, although when I hear a bird whistling I think of him. Which is only right – ain't it?

The local paper carried the following story:

Trade Fair at Monastery

An added attraction is a Yoga show given by Omani and Marvita who have been performing at Hastings this summer. On Wednesday, whilst Omani lowered himself into a black coffin and was covered by 5 cwt of sand, his son was undergoing an operation for appendicitis in a Hastings Hospital. After the last shovelful of sand had been shot on his head, Omani was seen to struggle and was hurriedly dug out by an assistant and Marvita. The sand, he explained, was wet; and the weight of it too great. The object of the act was for him to stay under the sand for five minutes. The act takes place only a few yards from the spot where a monk is reputed to have been buried alive centuries ago.

THE LIVING
GUY

tomorrow night Hastings' own escapologist "Omani" will be chained and padlocked to a stake on top of the Ore and Clive Vale bonfire boys' fire and will attempt to escape as the fire blazes. Here he is seen "taking it over" with one of the giant guys who will be on the fire with him.

A GENTLEMAN BY the name of Guy Fawkes (pronounced Fox but without, I regret, the same amount of animal cunning) decided in the year 1605 to blow up the Houses of Parliament and rather stupidly made a blunder of it. This has ever since had the most amazing psychological effect on the otherwise stolid British public, who may we mention are notorious for 'stiff upper lips' and championing the underdog, always providing of course that there is something to be gained out of it. Unfortunately for Mr Fawkes he was not the type of underdog that the public felt like championing, in fact the more they thought about his puny efforts in trying to blow up the Houses of Parliament, the more angry they became. They apparently still are, so to show their disapproval to Mr Fawkes, who surely by now must be past caring anyway, each year they work themselves up into an expansive mass hysteria by lighting bonfires all over the country. At the same time pounds' worth of fireworks are sent hurtling into the sky, effigies of Mr Fawkes are placed on top of bonfires and reduced to ashes, while with gleeful anticipation people of all ages and sizes stand around their respective bonfires watching the embarrassed Mr Guy Fawkes burn, while they themselves get red faces and scorched eyebrows, together with cold feet and frozen posteriors. Certain shopkeepers may reap a harvest out of all this and probably do, but when the following morning arrives the story is rather different: during the night fire brigades have been unusually busy, haystacks have been burnt to the ground and buildings found smouldering. Much worse still, animals have bolted for their lives in panic or have been stifled by the smoke. Fingers have been blown off and eyesights lost. Even tually when it is all over, a smattering of offenders will be gathered together in the local court, whereupon the magistrates will be heard to repeat their famous and much-worn phrase that 'This sort of thing has got to stop' whereupon everything is promptly forgotten until the next Guy Fawkes night, when of course it happens all over again, ad nauseam.

One can see from this that the said Mr Fawkes really started something, and some people may wonder whether a lot of suffering and nervous disorders may not have been saved and indeed expense, in later years, had he succeeded in his original mission.

Now, although this wicked but versatile gentleman has been the medium in making me jump out of my skin on numerous occasions and has also been the instigator of many sleepless nights, he did however give me the idea for a very good stunt. The stunt was this: that I should take his place on top of a bonfire and become a human living guy.

As I saw it, this stunt would have to be staged as follows: I would be chained or tied to the stake on top of a twenty-five foot high bonfire, and as the bonfire blazed I would attempt to escape. Let's face it, this could be a very dangerous escape and was therefore just up my street. I came to the conclusion that it should be possible to effect an escape as the flames shot up all around me, which to say the least of it should look very spectacular. I went to work on the plan and worked it out in every detail or at least so I thought, but I had not allowed in my calculations for the stupidity of some of the spectators, as will be seen.

Now one of the biggest bonfire celebrations takes place annually in the marketplace of the Sussex town called Battle, and so it was to this little historic town I found myself travelling in search of the Bonfire Boys Association. Eventually I found these people and put my idea to them. They in turn informed me kindly but firmly, as if I were a backward child, which of course once upon a time I had been, that it was too dangerous and that they could not permit it. But another association, known as the Ore and Clive Vale Bonfire Boys Association had other ideas. They welcomed the idea of me as a living guy, irrespective of whether I was simple or not, for this would undoubtedly draw the crowds and swell their takings. A meeting was called forthwith and it was agreed there and then that the Great Omani (Escapologist) would become a living Guy Fawkes and he would attempt to escape from a twenty-five foot high bonfire on Guy Fawkes Night in front of the crowds.

We were very lucky with the advance publicity on this particular stunt. Several newspapers carried the story and one week before the event I appeared on BBC Television at the Hammersmith Riverside Studios, London. The programme was that well-known feature *In Town Tonight* and at that time it was being televised. This was an enormous bit of luck and advance publicity for me because I was being interviewed mainly in connection with my forthcoming bon-fire escape bid. Perhaps in some respects I am a rather unusual person: possibly for that reason they decided to interview me in a rather unusual way. I was suspended upside down from the ceiling by a pulley, hanging by my legs, and thus possibly became the first man to be interviewed on television whilst hanging upside down.

On my arrival back in Hastings I discussed in detail with the Ore and Clive Vale Bonfire Boys Committee how the bonfire should be built. It would be twenty-five feet high; on top of it there would be a small platform for me to stand on through which a stake would run down to the ground. I should, of course, be tied to the stake. The bonfire would gradually slope off so that a concealed scaffold board would be there for me to run down once I had freed myself. Also, half a dozen of the bonfire boys were to be there standing by with a strong blanket to catch me fire brigade-wise in case I had to jump for it. There was to be a spotlight shining on the bonfire and the whole bonfire was to be ringed on the outside edges with petrol. This way, the outside of the bonfire would blaze first and burn in-wards and I would be the centre of a large ring of fire. In addition to being effective, this arrangement would give me time to escape. Or so I hoped, anyway.

Eventually, Saturday night arrived and with it one of the heaviest downpours of rain of the year. Yes it rained hard, very hard: solidly all day and well into the evening. The actual site where the stunt was to be held was at a place called Rock Lane, Hastings, and dur-ing the afternoon cars and even charabancs with booked parties turned up. But as the rain continued to pour down and the grass became soggy and muddy many cars and charabancs turned home again, no doubt in the belief that the show would be cancelled.

I arrived that evening in plenty of time at Rock Lane and in spite of the bad weather conditions I noted that there were several hundred people there and certainly a large number of teenagers. On my arrival I was soon spotted and people began to point me out to their friends. 'That's 'im,' said one, 'that's Omani.' Someone called out 'Good luck, mate'; two youngsters rushed forward with rain drenched paper for an autograph; others clapped, some whistled, whilst from others there was an occasional catcall. Squibs were being thrown everywhere; bangs going off all over the place and it seemed evident that the youngsters were determined not to let the rain dampen their ardour.

My experience in showbusiness generally has taught me that crowds vary greatly in their behaviour. Some are sporting and good-humoured while others can be rude and often violent and out for trouble whatever happens. I can usually sum up a crowd in a few seconds: perhaps it's a form of crowd psychology I've learnt. I had a strong suspicion that this particular crowd looked like being very unruly: I wasn't far wrong. However, my biggest shock came when I saw the bonfire which had been built for me and the general set-up. Hardly anything had been done in the way I planned it. The bonfire was twenty-five feet high all right but instead of being built on a slope as I had instructed, it was a sheer drop down. The spotlights that they had produced were two rusty old borrowed lamps from the railway, whilst the platform that had been erected for me was far too small and stuck up at an awkward angle. A large rope was supposed to be staked into the ground to keep the crowds from getting too near. Some teenagers had other ideas for it and were having a tug of war with the rope.

I climbed up the ladder to examine the bonfire more closely under the flickering lamps. The more I saw of it, the more I disliked it. In no way had it been built to my specifications. Still, it was too late to turn back now. Already, seeing me on the bonfire the excited crowd had rushed forward, circling round it. 'Come on mate, 'urry up,' cried one. 'What are you waiting for?' 'Yes, what's the matter? Got cold feet? Come on, burn 'im,' shouted another youth. 'Hurrah!' shouted another section of the crowd, 'Good old Omani, set him on fire!' It seemed to me as if pandemonium had broken loose. Some were yelling 'Cold feet!' others 'Burn him!'; some hissed while others clapped; everybody was making some sort of noise. Having examined the bonfire I decided to climb down the ladder again in search of the bonfire boys. No sooner had I climbed a couple of rungs down the ladder when an angry cry broke out from all and sundry, which rapidly sent me shooting up the ladder again. This gave rise to another outburst of 'Cold feet, get on with it,' and I was relieved to see that the bonfire boys had suddenly arrived and that we were ready to start.

One chap was detailed to tie and chain me to the stake, another was to put the petrol round and light the bonfire while others stood by with a blanket to catch me when I jumped, assuming that I escaped in time. Eventually my wrists were chained and padlocked in front of me while thirty yards of rope was coiled around my body, fixing me to the stake. He did his job well and the audience must have been impressed but in spite of this they yelled, roared and generally behaved like an unruly mob, which of course they were. I found myself wondering whether the crowds had changed so much since the days when witches were burnt in public.

Anyway, the time had come to start. 'I'm ready,' I shouted, 'ring the bonfire with petrol.' But the gentleman who was in charge of this part of the operation yelled back, 'Ain't got none.' 'What do you mean,' I shouted, 'ain't got none?' 'Well, the petrol,' he replied, 'is locked up in a shed and Tom's got the key, and Tom ain't turning up.' This was very clearly the signal for a fresh outburst of anger from the audience and I was loudly booed as 'Fake!' and 'Put-up job!'. This was backed up by fireworks whizzing angrily past my nose, too close for my liking. Another one landed on my leg and fell spluttering onto the faggots and fizzled out. 'But,' continued the man, 'we've got plenty of oil: that will do as well.' A drum of oil was hastily poured round the edge of the bonfire. The big moment had come to light it. The crowd had become silent: this was what they had been waiting for. I could see a mass of white faces staring up in the dark, eagerly watching and waiting. Suddenly someone cried out 'Good luck,' but was promptly howled down by the masses. I thought again that only a hundred and five years ago the last witches had been burnt in this country and although there was every likelihood of my escaping, in those days they weren't even given a sporting chance, and again I wondered whether the crowds had changed all that much in the years or whether deeper down there still lingered a great deal of sadism.

Silence fell over the mob again as the torch was lit. Everybody was tense. Although I was securely bound and chained, I had quickly summed the situation up and knew that I could escape in seven seconds. I also knew that I must not escape too soon, not before there was a reasonable blaze; on the other hand I dare not leave it too late for I knew from past experiences and mistakes that one or two seconds too long in the flames can be very painful. Some of the ropes that had been tied could quite easily be slipped, but not all: there were definitely knots which would have to be untied. I decided to leave the escape to the last minute, then work like lightning. I do not think there is an escapologist anywhere who is quicker at getting out of ropes than myself, so I was fairly confident. Nevertheless, split-second timing was essential otherwise there might indeed be a nasty accident. The suspense was terrific: it usually is in this business. But I knew I wouldn't have long to wait. Once I started the escape, fear would be forgotten... but oh, that waiting. Suddenly the bearer of the torch shouted 'Ready...' I croaked something back in reply, and dramatically he flung the lighted torch onto the bonfire. A cheer rang through the night. Everybody expected a big blaze of fire; everybody was disappointed. The torch hit the wet faggots, spluttered and went out. The crowd was angry and sent forth another howl of rage. 'What's the matter with yer? Light the ruddy fire!' And again he lit the torch and with much waving and show-manship hurled it at the uncooperative bonfire. It hit the damp wood, spluttered and again went out.

At this, the crowd were not slow in telling the bonfire boys and myself what they thought of Guy Fawkes in general and Omani in particular. The third try was luckier, although not for me. The oil caught, sending a large orange flame shooting into the air, singeing my nose and leaving in its wake a cloud of black smoke which cov-ered my face, making me look like an out-of-work minstrel. 'Hoo-ray! Hooray!' yelled the crowd. 'Bravo!' The large flame which had burnt so brilliantly and had been so instrumental in blacking my face and singeing my nose died down again and almost went out. 'Boo!' yelled the crowd. 'Boo!' But they were not to be outdone. A group of young men or boys hustled through the crowd, carrying something between them. As they came, the crowd melted away from them: then I saw the reason why. They were carrying a barrel of some highly inflammable spirit, and without more ado they flung it on the dying flame. With a roar, sparks and smoke leapt into the air and flames shot up everywhere, dangerously close to me. The crowd roared as the flames crackled and I knew my time had come to escape. Never have I worked so fast. I felt the heat of the flames near to me and getting more uncomfortable every second. As I un-tied the last knot, my fingers were sweating. My timing was perfect: I was free in seven seconds. Now it was time for me to jump, and be damn quick about it. 'Get ready,' I shouted, 'I'm coming.' Six of the bonfire boys held out an outstretched blanket for me to jump into. At least, I thought to myself, they have got this part of it right. Holding my arms up in the air, I made a spectacular leap from the top of the bonfire, through the flames, down … down… to be caught twenty-five feet below by the blanket. As I hit the blanket there was a tearing, ripping sound and it split in two, landing me with my head in the mud. And thus ended one of the most publicised fiascos it has been my misfortune to present.

Several newspapers covered the story before and after the event, with such headings as: Omani to Present Daring Escape, Ore Bonfire Challenge, Chained to Bonfire, One Guy to Another and so on. Indeed on this occasion I think the papers had been very kind to me, and two of them gave the following accounts:

Chained to Bonfire

The heaviest downpour of rain for weeks drove hundreds of people away from Rock Lane, Hastings, where they had been waiting to see the Great Omani present his bonfire escape on Saturday. At nine pm Omani was chained and padlocked around the wrists and tied with 40 yards of rope to a stake on top of the bonfire. Oil was poured round the bonfire and it was then lit. Several minutes elapsed before Omani got free; not before some of the flames had come dangerously near to him. Omani then sprung from the bonfire to be caught in a blanket by the Ore and Clive Bonfire Boys.

Another account ran as follows:

He was not for Burning
Omani's escape thrills Ore crowd

Climax to the Guy Fawkes celebrations of the Ore and Clive Vale Bonfire Boys was the feat of the Great Omani, the escapologist, at Rock Lane, on Saturday evening. Refused permission to carry out his act at the Battle celebrations, he climbed the ladder to the top of a 25 foot pyre. Standing on a platform, he was securely pinioned to a post and his hands were manacled. Then came the great moment. The bonfire was lit and several hundred men women and children settled down in a mass fit of trepidation to see whether Omani was for burning. One child near me (writes an Observer reporter) buried its face against its mother; and one or two women asked rather apprehensively whether Omani would be able to get away. Meanwhile, the object of their anxiety swayed backwards and forwards against the post, struggling dramatically with his manacles. Suddenly came the climax... or anti-climax? A section of the pyre caught; flames licked up to within a short distance of Omani and before you could say 'Guy Fawkes', his manacles were off and he was uncoiling the strands which hitherto held him so securely.

Roars of Applause

He gathered them, together with the manacles, and descended the ladder to a roar of applause, which for a few seconds drowned the crackling of the flames.

FRIDAY THE
13TH

OFTEN TO THE exasperation of managers and theatre owners all over the world, the Great Houdini always refused to perform on Friday the thirteenth. Many a theatre had to cancel his appearance on this date. That would undoubtedly mean, if Houdini was performing, losing a full house, because he was always top of the bill in his day, and not surprisingly the highest paid vaudeville artist. What is surprising is that a man of his intelligence should be superstitious to this degree. As has been stated by me on several occasions during interviews on radio and television, I can see no scientific or logical reason why Friday the thirteenth should be any different from any other day. Houdini, in all his wisdom, gave me an idea, however. Perhaps, one should say, a ready made story. I'd decided to perform a dangerous stunt on Friday the thirteenth, the day, I was not slow to point out to the media, that the Great Houdini would never perform on. This surely would interest them and they took the bait.

Southern Television decided to make quite a big thing out of the stunt and it was arranged that I should perform the following on the coming Friday the thirteenth: first they would film me having breakfast during which time I would accidentally (on purpose) spill the salt. Before leaving the house a mirror would be broken. Outside the house there was a painter on top of a ladder; I was to walk under the ladder. The painter would then drop his paint pot, just missing my head. I had no reason to disagree with any of this, especially the last part. Finally they would drive me to the edge of a hundred foot cliff, about half a mile past Roedean girls' school. Here would be taken the supreme risk of standing on my head on the extreme edge of the cliff and let the demons and goblins do their worst. My memory is none too brilliant, but the memory of much of that morning still lingers.

It was a house in Washington Street, Brighton, where we were to meet to do the first part of the filming. Having been introduced to the television crew it was agreed – sorry, ordered by the director – that first we would have the breakfast scene. Here I would spill the salt and presumably forget to throw it over my left shoulder with my right hand. All of which would delight the demons and goblins and from that moment make me a marked man. In short, to use a little modern day language, from that moment the devil would have a contract out on me. I sat down to breakfast to a palatable bacon and eggs.

The director explained to me at great length, which was entirely unnecessary, that I was to eat the bacon and eggs and after a few mouthfuls I was to knock over the salt, sending the devil into fits of ecstasy. Now to eat a few mouthfuls of bacon and eggs and to knock over a salt cellar did not require the acting expertise of Richard Burton, but the director seemed to think that it did. We rehearsed it and I swallowed mouthfuls of bacon and eggs, all of which pleased me very much as I was starving. Finally the director was satisfied. Over the years my experience of most directors is this: the only difference between God and a film director is that God can walk on water.

Swallowing a few more mouthfuls I stretched for the napkin and in doing so I knocked over the salt. 'Cut... cut!' shouted the director, 'That's fine, no retakes.' We had successfully completed stage one. 'Next,' said the director, adjusting slightly the halo on his head, 'we will do the mirror smashing sequence.' This surely would be even easier than the egg and bacon scene but possibly not so tasty.

'Here is a mirror,' said the director in a loud voice, pointing at an object that could be nothing else. 'Listen everybody. Omani is going to have a shave in the mirror, cut himself and pretend to then take it out on the mirror by smashing it.' Here again, this did not take the great acting ability of Richard Harris or Oliver Reed. Though possibly I could have learnt a thing or two about smashing mirrors from Oliver Reed. Never in my life have I been able to learn a script: thank heavens we didn't need one now. That is why actors and actresses amaze me with their brilliant memories. How they can possibly learn line after line and memorise them leaves me dumbfounded.

The cameras were on me as I stood in front of the mirror, covering my face with lather. This did not need rehearsing. It was time to start shaving. 'Now, now!' yelled the director. This was to be my big acting moment. I was to pretend to cut myself. Making an extra bold stroke with the razor, I jerked my head, giving it a half-turn accompanied by a suitable groan. The Richards Harris and Burton of this world would have been proud of me. It looked very realistic. It was: by mistake I'd cut my ruddy face. The little red trickles on the white foam proved this. 'Cut…cut!' shouted the director. 'How right you are,' I replied.

'Now the ladder sequence,' said sir. 'Are you OK, Omani?' We hadn't quite stopped the bleeding but we were on the way. 'After the next one we'll take a break,' said the director. I was disappointed. I was hoping he would say 'Take ten…'

'This sequence is easy,' said the director. 'Come with me.' We walked together down the hall and out through the front door. He suddenly stopped and pointed and said, 'Look.' I stopped. After all, if a director says look, you look. There sure enough, about two houses away was a ladder with a painter on top: he seemed to be painting the top of the house. 'Now,' said sir, 'you are going to walk along the pavement and under the ladder. The painter is then going to drop his pot of paint, just missing your head. Now what do you think of that? Don't worry,' he continued, 'he knows what he's doing, you'll be quite safe.' 'If he doesn't,' I retorted, 'we'll be on the six o'clock news as well, but what an undignified way to go. Being hit on the head by a pot of paint on Friday the thirteenth.' So it was decided that I would walk slowly towards the ladder and then under it. The painter would then let his pot of paint go, missing my head. The camera was in position across the road, ready to pick me up. As usually happens when filming out of doors, a small crowd quickly gathered. The old clapper board went 'smack' and I started to walk slowly towards the ladder and then under it. Just as I got to the other side there was the sound of something crashing as it hit the ground.

The painter and the paint pot had done their job well. I hoped there would be no need for a retake. There wasn't. 'Alright everybody, that's fine,' shouted the director, 'We'll have a break.' 'He meant,' I said, turning to the audience, 'Take ten.' No reason why we shouldn't pretend we are in Hollywood.

So far on this Friday the thirteenth we had spilt salt, smashed a mirror, walked under a ladder and slightly cut my face. The good news was that I had been eating lots of eggs and bacon. But the big one was yet to come. Having had our break it was time to say goodbye to Washington Street and head for the coast. In particular for the hundred foot cliff just past Roedean girls' school where I would attempt to stand on my head on the extreme edge. This particular stretch of cliff was ideal for camera angles. Below, the waves crashed onto the beach, drawing the shingle back into the sea. Above, seagulls screeched as they dived only to rise swiftly again as if on some invisible giant switchback and disappear out to sea gliding on a gust of wind. Cameramen from various newspapers had been waiting for us at the cliff top. Most of them I knew from previous stunts and we all got on very well together. It is surprising and yet very understandable that so many people are afraid of heights. To go within a foot of the edge of a hundred foot cliff and ask someone to look down would frighten most people. Tell them that you are going to stand on your head on the edge of that cliff and they will usually reply, 'I wouldn't do it for a thousand pounds,' which is probably as well as they would never live to enjoy it.

So the final shots for the television film were in sight. A fence runs along the top of the cliff about three feet from the edge – a sensible safety precaution. The only things that can be seen on the other side of the fence are rabbits, seagulls, butterflies, and on certain Fridays the Great Omani.

The director went up to the fence and looked over. He saw and heard the waves crashing against the beach below, which seemed a long way down. He quickly came back, looking a little worried. 'Are you sure you will be alright, Omani? You don't have to do it if you're not.' The man had a heart after all. 'Look, you don't have to go right to the edge to do it, and perhaps you should have a lifeline around you.' 'Don't worry,' I said. 'I can stand on my head better than I can sometimes stand on my feet. Especially when I've had a bottle of wine washed down with a few cognacs.' He took a sly look at the cliff again and announced that he could do with a brandy. 'Any-way,' I announced, 'I won't be right at the edge of the cliff.' The colour slowly came back to his cheeks. 'Thank heavens,' he said. 'At last, Omani you are beginning to show some sense. How far from the edge will you be? About a foot?' 'No,' I replied, 'about four inches.' The colour slowly left his cheeks again.

First of all we had a few interviews sitting near the cliff edge: these were mostly for television and radio. Eventually the time came for the stunt. The cameras were now in position, picking me up on the cliff's edge. The director gave a loud clap from the clapper board, more from fear than anything else, not that it made a difference, for in a stunt like that I take my own time. Slowly, very slowly, I stretched my feet upwards towards the heavens, swaying slightly as they pointed towards the vast expanse of sky. At last my feet were pointing straight to heaven, and I had to be damn careful or I would follow them, and as far as I know, St Peter is not yet ready for me. There appears to be a housing shortage there as well. As I remained upside down, my feet and body swayed slightly in the wind. I like to give good value for money. A minute, maybe a minute and a half, I don't remember, but eventually my legs returned to the ground. Not before, however, the seagulls which had been circling overhead had given me their message of good luck in their own particular way. The small audience who had gathered, and indeed the reporters who had gathered, gave me a round of applause. This was nice of them, and goes to show that even reporters can be human at times. Suddenly, one of the reporters, who is a freelance and does a lot of work for the nationals, came running up in a bit of a panic. 'Ron,' he said, 'I'm awfully sorry, but could I ask you to do it again? Just for a few seconds. I forgot I hadn't got any film in the camera and I haven't got any pictures.' 'Of course,' I said. So once again I found myself and my legs pointing heaven-wards. All of which gave everybody a chance to have a second shot. A chance which the gulls were not slow to take advantage of.

So Friday the thirteenth passed without incident, except for the slight nick received while shaving. In fact, in some ways it was a lucky day for me. Possibly due to the timely intervention of the seagulls. Oh, there I go again, getting superstitious.

That evening we watched and relived it all again on television. Frankly, I was quite proud of myself as an actor. After it was all over I turned to my friends and in my most impressive Shakespearean voice I asked, 'What has Richard Burton got that I haven't?'

Their reply, regrettably, is unprintable. Ignorant clots.

ROYAL
PAVILION
BRIGHTON

It's just a light (bulb) snack

THE MOUNTAIN WILL have to come to Mohammed,' I said, laying down the letter and envelope that I had just opened. 'What on Earth are you talking about?' said Marvita, 'and who's that letter from?' 'The producer of the radio magazine *Today* suggests I come to London to talk over the possibility of my appearing on their breakfast magazine. They want the broadcast to take the form of an interview and the idea of my eating an electric light bulb during the interview appears to greatly appeal to them.' 'You know,' I said, 'the BBC seem to have an insane desire, whenever they see me, to fill me full of glass. I have eaten no less than six bulbs for them on various occasions.' 'Are you going?' asked Marvita. 'I haven't the time,' I said, 'after all, I'm doing about six or seven shows a day on the West Pier, how can I fit it in? If they want me they will have to come down here and take a recording.'

My reply to the BBC was just that. This piece of cheek on my part was answered, much to my surprise, by their agreeing. However, instead of a recording, they wanted to make a live broadcast from their new BBC studio, recently opened at the Royal Pavilion, Brighton.

It was a couple of days before the BBC announcer Bob Gunnell came down to see me. We soon became friendly and discussed the forthcoming interview. He decided he would like to hear the sound effect of eating an electric light bulb, so would I mind eating one? Once again I weighed into my transparent meal. Finally, it was arranged that I should broadcast on the following morning at 7.15

and, if we were lucky, there would be a repeat at 8.15. Bob would pick me up at 6.30 by car and we would be there at 6.40, in plenty of time.

Eventually, Monday morning arrived and, true to his word, Bob's car pulled up at my door at 6.30am sharp and soon we were speeding towards the Royal Pavilion. It was indeed a glorious morning, with a brilliant blue sky and the Royal Pavilion, surrounded by a mass of exotic summer flowers and neatly kept lawns, soon greeted us. The birds were singing beautifully, as if they hadn't a care in the world – which they probably hadn't – and indeed we might have been in the heart of the country, one hundred years earlier. I had passed through the grounds of the Royal Pavilion before, but on this early September morning it seemed at its best, in all its serenity, in all its beauty and regality. For a few minutes I forgot all about the broadcast in the midst of all this splendour.

I felt happy in this atmosphere. I could well understand how it was a favourite place of the Prince Regent and with an imagination such as I have, it was not hard to turn back the calendar. How well I could picture the coaches going to and fro; the top hats and long elegant dresses; the picturesque coachmen and footmen; the curtseying and bowing, all of which went to make up the old-world charm.

Day dreams last but a short time and I was soon jerked out of my Regency dream by Bob banging on the main door. A few minutes went by before anybody came, but soon a shuffling noise told us someone was on the way. A man suddenly appeared. 'What do you want?' he called. 'We've come for the broadcast,' said Bob, 'will you let us in?' 'What broadcast?' said the man, 'I've heard nothing about any broadcast.' 'We're on the *Today* programme at 7.15.' 'You're not on today or any other day,' said the man, 'not without an entry permit. Those are my orders. No one gets into the Royal Pavilion without a permit.'

Wagging a stern looking finger in my direction, he continued, 'We've got thousands of pounds worth of stuff here, including the Regency silver and plate. Also some furniture and silver on loan from Buckingham Palace, all part of the Regency exhibition.' 'Good heavens,' said Bob, suddenly realising the position, 'the BBC have forgotten to send down our permits.' 'And,' I added, 'time is getting short.' 'Listen,' I said, 'I'm Omani. All I'm going to do is to have an interview with Bob Gunnell in the BBC studio here and eat an electric light bulb.' 'You're going to do what?' cried the startled security officer. 'Look,' I said, opening my briefcase, 'here's the bulb.' 'You're going to eat... that?' he retorted. 'Well not all of it,' I said modestly, 'but most of it I hope.' 'I believe,' said Bob, 'he thinks you're an escaped lunatic. Give me your contract a minute. Look, here's his contract, that should be proof enough.' The officer looked at Bob, then at me, then a nervous glance at his Regency silver, some of which could be seen in the background. Suddenly he seemed satisfied. The key turned in the door and we felt ourselves lucky to be inside the Royal Pavilion. 'This,' said the officer, 'this I must see.'

Bob went ahead quickly, and finding he had disappeared, the first thing I did was to take the wrong turning and get lost. This, I can assure you, was neither the time nor the place to get lost in. I found myself dodging in and out of tapestries, Regency furniture, numerous oil paintings and pieces of much guarded Regency silver which, under normal conditions, I should have loved to linger over. The thought of an infuriated security officer searching for me hurried me on in my search for Bob or the studio. Eventually – and much to my relief – I found both. The studio was small but furnished well and in excellent taste; needless to say, in strong Regency period. I looked out of the small latticed windows on to the lawns. I wondered what stories this small room could tell; of what memories it could speak. Stories of tragedy and sorrow – or perhaps of vast banquets and happiness? I hope so. If I could have told the Prince Regent, 'Sire, in years to come, a man will eat an electric light bulb in this room and all England will hear him by turning on the radio,' what would he have said, I wonder? Perhaps, 'Omani, what is an electric light bulb?' My thoughts were brought to an end when Bob said, 'London is coming through now,' for the Pavilion studio was worked by remote control. If the Prince Regent had said, 'What is remote control?' I think I would have to reply, 'Sire, I haven't the slightest idea!'

The two microphones were in place; we had one each. Bob adjusted his earphones and took a deep breath. Thirty seconds to go and we were on the air. Jack de Mario was introducing us from Broadcasting House, London, then Bob took over and the opening part of the broadcast ran something like this:

'...and the hungry gentleman who is with me is the Great Omani, and his breakfast, which he is enjoying with evident relish is – of all things – an electric light bulb. But I'm going to keep him hungry for a little longer. Omani, when I first met you, you were about to jump from the West Pier into the sea, ablaze with petrol; trussed up in a straitjacket and with your hands manacled. Stunts appear to be your profession.'

'Yes, they are indeed – and I have quite a few to my credit... there was the time when I travelled from Hastings to Piccadilly Circus entombed inside a block of concrete: a sort of human fossil, and again when I travelled the same route stripped to the waist, lying in an open coffin full of broken glass on the top of a car, in February. I've been buried alive in a coffin; hung upside down in a straitjacket from various high buildings; escaped from blazing buildings for a film; ridden the Wall of Death and, oh, many other stunts...'

During this particular broadcast I felt completely at ease and, eventually, after more questions and answers I ate my electric light bulb, which was a wonderful sound effect over a microphone.

We had run over our time limit by thirty seconds which, in my opinion, was not too bad. Bob seemed very satisfied about the way we put it over. I think he had every reason to be, we were in fact very lucky to broadcast at all. I took a farewell look at the studio. I hoped secretly that it would not be the last time I would see it. I had become quite attached to the little studio and hoped that perhaps there might be another broadcast in the future. We came out to be met by the security officer. He seemed more affable and greeted us warmly not without, I noticed, eyeing my pockets to see if they were bulging with silver spoons! He was soon telling us his family history and more particularly his experiences as a regimental sergeant-major. He was a grand type really, but I was in a hurry to get home and, indeed, to hear the repeat if there was to be one. If it was hard to get into the Royal Pavilion without a permit, it was considerably harder to get out of it and not until I had heard a great deal about military life in general and sergeant-majors in particular.

Once again I was home and as I always manage to forget something – this time the key – I knocked on my door. My wife, who was still in bed, answered, 'Who is it?' 'It's me,' I retorted, 'Ronald "Royal Pavilion" Omani, I haven't got a permit, but will you let me in?' The door opened and she let me in.

A few hours later, Marvita and I were performing once again on the West Pier when two reporters came to interview me, complete with camera. Seven hours later, the *Evening Argus* carried the following story, complete with pictures:

It's Just a Light (Bulb) Snack

The chap having a light bulb snack for the benefit of the BBC listeners is forty year old Brighton stuntman Omani. He did it today in the new Royal Pavilion studio after a chat with interviewer Bob Gunnell on the early morning programme *Today*. Omani, who jumps in chains from Brighton West Pier into a sea of blazing petrol seven or eight times daily, says he loves the work. But his three children are not following his profession. The light bulb stunt? 'It's quite genuine,' says the man with the cast-iron stomach, 'I break them up and swallow them. The crowds love it!'

A SALUTE TO
HOUDINI

Going going gone!

ONCE IT WAS my privilege to meet an elderly gentleman in his late seventies, by the name of Bert Croyle. In his early days he had worked in London as head electrician in many of the big variety theatres. He had worked with many famous artists and vaudeville stars of yesterday. He knew the famous Ching Ling Soo, who met an untimely death on stage when presenting the 'catching a bullet in the mouth' trick. He also knew and had worked with the legendary Great Houdini. He told me that Houdini was a very pleasant and polite man to work with, though conceited and at times very temperamental. But then what great artist isn't temperamental? During his tour of England, it appears Houdini had visited Brighton and had appeared top of the bill at the Brighton Hippodrome. Sadly, like many other theatres, the Hippodrome is now a Bingo Hall. Only the ghosts of yesterday tread the boards to the phantom music of bygone days. One day, Bert Croyle and I were sitting down sipping a glass of wine when he suddenly said, 'You know, I actually saw Houdini perform his famous death jump from West Pier. This was a publicity stunt to advertise his show at the Brighton Hippodrome. He was handcuffed, chained and padlocked and jumped from the pier into the sea and escaped underwater in about two minutes. The pier was packed. What a showman he was that night. As always with Houdini, the theatre was sold out.' I asked Bert how long ago it was that Houdini performed on the West Pier. 'About fifty years ago,' he replied. 'Right,' I said, 'you've just given me an idea for my next stunt. I will perform Houdini's jump from where he performed it on the West Pier, with handcuffs and chains, as he performed it fifty years ago. I will present it as a salute to the memory of the world's all time greatest escapologist.' This was a very good story and I had agreed to sell it to a well known London agency called *Features International* as an exclusive. The morning before the stunt was due to take place, Bert Croyle and I had an interview with one of the BBC radio stations and we discussed the forthcoming stunt. One question the interviewer asked Bert was 'Do you think that Omani is as good as Houdini? He has done some amazing things.' Bert hesitated, turned to me and asked what I thought. 'Simple,' I said, 'Houdini was the greatest of all time. Long after our names are forgotten he will still be a legend.' 'You may be right,' said Bert, 'but Omani is the best we have got today.' Several years had passed since I had performed on the West Pier. It had changed owners and now belonged to the Metropole Hotel, Brighton. The morning of the stunt arrived and Frank Durham, a director of *Features International*, and his camera-girl arrived to pick me up at my house. With my suitcase packed with manacles, chains and a pair of bathing trunks, I got into his car and we headed for the West Pier.

On arrival we were in for a shock. A battery of about a dozen cameramen and reporters were waiting for us. A gathering of the media such as one might expect had the rumour got around that Dolly Parton was going to appear topless! Suddenly we realised that they had found out through our BBC broadcast. I apologised to Frank, saying I would try to get rid of them. Most of my life I had been trying to get the national press to come to my stunts. Now I found myself trying to get rid of them. This was right out of character. I was rather like some film star covering up her face at Gatwick Airport, pretending she did not want publicity but making damn sure she got it. This would probably be the only time in my life I would turn my back on a camera. It was obvious they had no intention of going away; they had come for my pictures and intended to get them. They soon pointed out, quite correctly, they had as much right to be on the pier as I had. It was hopeless. I told Frank they would not go away. Sportingly he said, 'Then let's join forces.' As this was the middle of summer, the pier was packed with excited holiday-makers. Several years earlier, my lovely wife Eileen and I had performed many times on the pier, when I used to perform underwater escapes four or five times a day. So there was nothing new to me in all this.

The pier master, Roy Royston, had insisted that the lifeguards and beach boat should be present in case something went wrong. He had a diving stage rigged up for me on the pier and on the beach. Changing, I carried my handcuffs and chains and mounted the diving stage to get ready for the jump. There was one big snag: the sea was rough. This did not worry me at all. I had performed in much rougher seas. The trouble was, was it too rough for them to launch the beach lifeboat? Time and time again they launched it and time and time again the waves crashed into it, flinging it back onto the beach, often turning it over. If they could launch it and get it away from the beach they would be all right. Getting it out off the beach was the hard part. It was decided to postpone the stunt for one hour in the hope that the sea would calm down a bit. Eventually there was a lull and the lifeboat was launched with two lifeguards in it. One of the lifeguards was an old friend of mine, David Bunch. As head lifeguard for some years on Brighton beach, it can be said that there are many people walking about who owe their lives to him. At a time like this, David is a useful chap to have around.

The whole length of the side of the pier was black with people waiting to see the jump. As I stood on the diving stage, crowds pressed round. Crowds were also gathering on the beach. I wondered to myself whether fifty years ago the scene had been much the same when Houdini had stood here, chained and handcuffed, waiting to jump in the sea. I also wondered if the sea had been as rough on that day. Quite a few wise cracks were passing between the audience and myself. It lessens tension. Soon they had finished chaining and handcuffing me. They had done a very good job. Not many people thought that I could escape out of that lot on land, never mind underwater. I was now standing on the diving stage ready to take the plunge. The lifeboat was hovering off the pier riding the large waves comfortably, the lifeguards looking a little worried. The cameras were all in position ready to catch me as I took the plunge down into the sea, forty feet below, just as Houdini had done fifty years earlier. *The Mirror, The Express* and many others waited with their cameras. Suddenly there was a stir in the crowd. I heard a voice shouting, 'Make way! Make way!' I looked to see what all the commotion was about and saw a large figure heading towards me. He wore a black cloak lined with red. In his hand he held a smart silver topped ebony walking stick. His flowing red beard told me that my old pal, Professor Pat Cullen, had arrived just in the nick of time. His tim-

101

ing, like mine, was always spot on whenever cameras were around. The professor mounted the stage and took charge of the proceedings as he usually did. He told the gaping crowd that they were lucky to be able to witness the modern Houdini (me) and that he, Professor Cullen, would predict that no accident would befall the Great Omani on this occasion. He then whispered into my ear not to take a long time as the beer was already poured out. He then made a dramatic exit back to the bar, but, I hasten to add, not before he had made sure the cameras had seen him. Finally, to the chorus of '5-4-3-2-1-jump!' I jumped, making a perfect landing into a big wave and disappeared underwater with my friends the fish, who I swim with during the day and eat at night but they don't know this. I remained underwater for about ninety seconds and surfaced again, free of my shackles.

It was nice to look up and see hundreds of happy faces applauding me. It was nice to see the national press taking pictures. It was nice to be able to honour the Great Houdini after fifty years. It was very nice to be able to slide back into the pier bar, for the last time, and to find my old friend Professor Cullen and the press had the drinks lined up for me.

Next day, the following articles appeared in the papers, together with some quite sensational pictures:

Daily Mirror

Going, Going, Gone

Stuntman Ron Cunningham had the holiday crowd gasping yesterday. He stood on the West Pier, Brighton, hooded and locked in chains. Then he jumped into fifteen foot deep water. It took him only ninety seconds to free himself and bob triumphantly on the surface, where he was rescued by lifeguards. Ron, a fifty-five year old grandfather, otherwise known as 'The Great Omani', was repeating a death dive performed by Houdini at the same spot fifty years ago. Stuntman Ron does have a strange liking for doing funny things beside the seaside. He was last seen demonstrating his enthusiasm for the Common Market by hanging upside down from a cliff at Beachy Head.

Daily Express

Three pictures appeared in the above newspaper with the following write up:

Fifty Years Ago to the Day, Ron's Dive in Honour of Houdini.

Well, it's one way of remembering an anniversary. Escape artist Ron Cunningham made a big splash of honouring his hero, Houdini, yesterday. He got himself all trussed up and leapt from the West Pier at Brighton just like the great man himself did fifty years ago. Having roped in his son to bind him hand and foot, sixty year old Ron popped his head in a hood just to make things more difficult. Then he hobbled to the end of a platform and took the plunge watched by admiring holiday-makers.

Triumphant

He surfaced quickly, bottom side up and a minute later he'd got his head above water again and was triumphantly waving his shackles in the air. After his ducking, Ron, whose stage name is 'The Great Omani', said, 'I've been doing most of Houdini's stunts for twenty years and couldn't let this day go by without doing something special.' Houdini himself would surely have applauded Ron's slick feat. But then he knew better that anyone that you can't keep a good man down for long.

IN WHICH I SAY GOODBYE

Are you like me? Not very good at saying goodbye? If you are, it's very human I suppose. Although we have never met, I feel strangely sorry that I've got to say goodbye to you. We have been friends through the entire length of this book and for this I thank you. We are, I suppose, just two more ships that passed in the night. So instead of saying goodbye to you, may I shout that well-known and depressing clarion call... TIME LADIES AND GENTLEMEN, PLEASE, Hurry along now. Because, you see, *The Crowd Roars* has come to its end. Another reason: I am getting pretty ancient myself. So I have to hurry to make sure I live long enough to finish the last chapter. This is before the gentleman with the shiny top hat, and equally shiny Daimler arrives to take me to the happy hunting ground of all stuntmen. A jovial place, I assume, where we can crash cars, fall off buildings and have non-stop bar fights to our hearts' content...

So, Time Ladies and Gentlemen, please. Perhaps someday someone will come up to me and say, 'Hello, I read your book.' Oh yes, it's possible that someone somewhere might read it one day. If you do, I hope you don't ask for your money back. My ego would never stand it.

But before we part, what better idea than for me to go to my little cellar and find a decent bottle of wine. Today and for this special occasion, a German wine I think. How about a bottle of Blue Nun? An excellent wine which must be neither shaken nor stirred.

I raise my glass... to you... thank you and goodbye.

ABOUT OMANI

Ronald Charles Elliot Cunningham was born on the 10th July, 1915. His place of birth was at the family home and estate, Horton Manor, Horton, Bucks. At his birth he became fourth hereditary lord of the manor. He had an elder sister, Joy; they were very close. Much of his childhood and teens were spent at the Georgian Manor House in its beautiful and extensive grounds. He had a very happy childhood. His first prep school was at St George's School, Windsor Castle. His second was Rimpton at Broadstairs in Kent and from there he went on to his public school, Sherborne. At fifteen, his mother died; a severe blow as they were very close. She was a lady greatly loved by all the villagers. After leaving school, he travelled to France, Germany and Spain, training for the family business of wine-shipping. His father married again in his seventies but died soon after. Horton Manor had been sold and after his father's death the family business and money disappeared. Suddenly, at a very low ebb in his life the miracle happened. A book fell at his feet, its title *The Secrets of Houdini*. From that moment the Great Omani was born. Omani was very happily married for 35 years before his wife and partner died. They had three children.

ABOUT THE CULLENS

Patrick Cullen

Patrick Cullen was born in Ireland, his parents being a song and dance act. At the age of fourteen he ran away from home and joined the army, enlisting in the Prince of Wales Dragoon Guards. He served in India, China and Burma. Whilst in the Far East, he studied palmistry, astrology and some of the mysteries of the East. He also fought in the Spanish Civil War. He appears to have been well-decorated with medals. He met his wife, Margaret, on the pleasure beach in Blackpool. She was also very interested in palmistry and clairvoyance. They teamed up as palmists. Patrick Cullen became known as the 'Professor'. He has read the palms of many famous British and Hollywood stars of his era. A large picture of the Professor reading the palm of Jane Mansfield still hangs on the wall of his home. Professor Cullen, who died in the early eighties, was a famous and flamboyant character. He also appeared in a number of films, including *Oh! What a Lovely War*. Whilst in the army, he rose to the rank of regimental sergeant major. His nickname in the army was 'Dynamite'. That says it all.

Margaret Cullen

From an early age Margaret showed signs of clairvoyant gifts. She was also gifted with a good singing voice: a dramatic soprano. She became three times winner of the famous radio show The Carrol Levis Discoveries. Margaret also won two certificates from the Royal School of Music. She has written a number of poems, some of which have been published. Margaret's main interests, however, were clairvoyance and palmistry. She also studied yoga. As a clairvoyant, she has had clients from all over the world. Author of this book, Omani, says ... 'In her presence I often feel a spiritual aura of protection which I cannot explain scientifically. A truly remarkable lady.' Margaret still practises her palm readings in Brighton.

ABOUT THIS BOOK

This book was made by Danny Birchall, Steve Hill, Sheena Macdonald, Maggie Haynes and the late Deb Thomas.

Acknowledgements: Cover photo by Nils Hefner. Photos on pages 13, 41, 53 (by Terry Connolly), 57 and 89 courtesy of The Evening Argus. The photo on page 13 appeared in The World's Fair. Photos on p 79 (by Geoffrey Day) and p 97 (by David McEnery), courtesy of the Daily Mirror.

Articles appeared courtesy of The Evening Argus, the Brighton and Hove Leader, the Bognor Regis Observer, the Sussex Express and County Herald, the Daily Mirror and the Daily Express.

Printed by Digaprint Ltd, Hollingdean Road, Brighton.

ISBN No: 0 904733 70 X

Copyright: © Ron Cunningham 1998

ABOUT QUEENSPARK

QueenSpark Books is a community writing and publishing group based in Brighton. We believe that everyone has a history and that anyone who wants to can be a writer. Our aim is to encourage and publish writing by people who do not normally get into print. QueenSpark Books is not a commercial company. We have two part-time paid workers, but the rest of us are volunteers who work together to write and produce books, gaining and sharing skills and confidence as we go.

We have several active writing workshops in Brighton and Hove. Our manuscript group reads all manuscripts that are sent to us and sets up book-making groups for those we decide to publish. All groups are run on a cooperative basis.

QueenSpark Books is a member of the national Federation of Worker Writers and Community Publishers. We can give you the addresses of other Federation groups and information on the books they publish.

QueenSpark Books gratefully acknowledges the support of South East Arts, the local council of Brighton and Hove, and the Foundation for Sport and the Arts.

If you would like more information about our activities, please contact:

QueenSpark Books
49 Grand Parade
Brighton
BN2 2QA
Tel/Fax (01273 571710)

BRIGHTON REFERENCE LIBRARY
CHURCH STREET
BRIGHTON BN1 1UE
TELEPHONE: 296969